TEACHING THE COMMONS

Teaching
the Commons

Place, Pride, and the
Renewal of Community

Paul Theobald

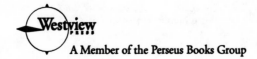
Westview
PRESS
A Member of the Perseus Books Group

Copyright © 1997 by Westview Press, A Member of the Perseus Books Group

Published in 1997 in the United States of America by Westview Press, 5500 Central Avenue, Boulder, Colorado 80301-2877, and in the United Kingdom by Westview Press, 12 Hid's Copse Road, Cumnor Hill, Oxford OX2 9JJ

Library of Congress Cataloging-in-Publication Data
Theobald, Paul, 1956–
  Teaching the commons : place, pride, and the renewal of community
/ Paul Theobald.
     p.   cm.
  Includes bibliographical references (p.   ) and index.
  ISBN 0-8133-2303-7 (hc). — ISBN 0-8133-2302-9 (pbk.)
  1. Education, Rural—Social aspects—United States—History.
2. Community and school—United States—History.   3. United States—
Rural conditions.   4. Sociology, Rural—United States—History.
I. Title.
LC5146.5.T54   1997
370'.973'091734—dc21   96-51814
                                                                      CIP

The paper used in this publication meets the requirements of the American National Standard for Permanence of Paper for Printed Library Materials Z39.48-1984.

10   9   8   7   6   5

*For the women with whom
I share a home:
Jan, Brianna, Renee,
and Alayna*

Contents

Acknowledgments

Renewing a sense of community, particularly in the countryside, is a cultural project that rests heavily on an educational foundation. Although the enemies of community are currently unseen, they need not remain so. This book was written to facilitate the kind of study required to make them visible. That is to say, it was written as a guide to be used by those who recognize that community restoration is a practical necessity in an age of dwindling natural resources, an age when democracy itself has been put on trial, an age when information has come to be controlled by huge multinational corporate interests. Such interests have co-opted the educational agenda of this country and have turned schooling into a process designed to meet their needs: to feed them with good workers, to make them globally competitive.

Education, of course, can be reconfigured so that it can help us conserve dwindling natural resources, nurture democracy, and put information to work in the creation of vital, vibrant communities. I hope that this book will show how the rural school can be fashioned to facilitate this rather large cultural project. If I have succeeded at all in this task, it is because of a wide array of friends and scholars, including Wendell Berry, David Orr, John Goodlad, Marty Strange, Wes Jackson, Paul Gruchow, Osha Gray Davidson, James Anderson, Craig Howley, Bruce Miller, and Alan DeYoung. They will likely recognize their influence in the pages that follow. A special thanks goes to Jim Fanning, Toni Haas, Paul Nachtigal, and Paul Olson for their helpful comments on earlier drafts of this book. Thanks, too, should go to Gaile Cannella, Carolyn Clark, Jim Lentz, Randy Parry, Dale Snauwaert, Ron Rochon, Mike Johnson, Larry Rogers, and Ed Mills for their words of encouragement and support as I tried to produce this book over and above the day-to-day demands of administrative work in the academy. Last, my sincere appreciation goes to Melissa Jockheck for her kind assistance with this manuscript.

Paul Theobald

Introduction

————

Real reforms are, in the beginning, impractical by definition.
—Paul Gruchow, 1996

This is a book about the role that schools can play in the promotion or, regrettably, the dissolution of community. The suggestions it contains apply to all types of schools in all kinds of locales. A central argument of the book is that wherever a school exists, the professionals who work within it must focus their pedagogical energy on the immediate place inhabited by the school; that is, they must make the word "local" in the phrase "local school" mean something if we are ever to be successful at elevating a sense of community in this society. In *Teaching the Commons* the reader will find systematic attention to the circumstances faced by rural schools, for that is what I know and that is, in many ways, who I am. The analysis used in this book, however, can illuminate and direct educational work in other contexts as well: urban or suburban, coastal town or border town, and so on.

This book is premised on two assumptions that I believe are well warranted. First, rural schools ought to have a place in the educational landscape of this country. They have an indispensable role to play. Second, schools ought to attend more consciously to their physical place on earth and the social, political, and economic dynamics that surround it. Doing so would render the entire school experience more meaningful and, in the process, would contribute in a small, though not insignificant, way to a cultural healing desperately needed in American society. We need to foster a sense that community is a valuable societal asset, something to be promoted rather than destroyed. Rural schools, through concerted pedagogical and curricular attention to the dynamics that impinge on their particular place, can rekindle community allegiance and can nurture that suppressed part of us that finds fulfillment in meeting community obligations.

By attending to their place, rural schools can begin to set a new institutional trajectory for formal education in this country. Rather than promoting a simplistic agenda that can be described accurately as equipping children with the factual knowledge needed by future employers, the global economy, or the Educational Testing Service, the school could become an agent for the restoration of community. It could do this, in part, by encouraging children to explore the wisdom inherent in elevating the common good above their own individual desires. This is an idea with a long intellectual tradition in the West, an idea that has been effectively buried in this country by our feverish consumer culture.

Because the arguments offered in this book are decidedly countercultural, they will appear to many to be impractical. "Everyone knows," for instance, that people prefer to live in large cities because there's more to do there. "Everyone knows" that people naturally crave money and desire as much of it as they can get. "Everyone knows," too, that businesses must stay focused on the bottom line. And on and on it could go. Although these ideas are culturally popular, the record of human history suggests that they are patently false.

Overcoming the power of these cultural beliefs, however, is no easy task. Yet this is precisely what is required of anyone who would seek substantive changes in the interest of a brighter future. To think that a democracy such as ours can be sustained without healthy communities requires the embrace of an inordinately weak definition of democracy. Those who have observed, recently, the growing disparities between rich and poor or the growing power of multinational corporations will concur that we are drifting in the direction of weak democracy at a pretty rapid clip. If we set our sights on the restoration of community—something within the reach of all of us—we will at the same time increase the odds for a stronger democracy and a better future.

But, again, it's a tall order, and this is why the restoration of communities must take place on an educational rather than, as in the past, an economic foundation. Those who would embrace the task of converting the local school into an agent of community renewal, transforming it from its (all-too-often) current role as unwitting contributor to community destruction, will need to meet culturally popular views with considerable intellectual sophistication. One predictable taunt is that the renewal advocate is "living in the past." The phrase is almost always uttered as an attempt to apply enough cultural force to shame anyone who shows signs of saying or listening to anything other than that which is considered conventional wisdom. It is difficult to resist this force. This book was written, in part, to enable the reader to construct the understanding necessary to muster such resistance and thus be able to render most of what passes for conventional wisdom powerless. In the process, a piece of the educational foundation upon which rural communities might be restored will have been put in place.

Since it's becoming popular today to suggest that the concept of community is too vague or too ambiguous to be helpful in the creation of public policy, Chapters 1–3 in Part One examine the kinds of ideas upon which community was built in the past. The very deep roots of what we consider conventional wisdom are also explored, an exercise that demonstrates how alternative historical trajectories would have led to far different ideas, such as schools operating for completely different purposes. In Part Two, Chapters 4–6 chronicle the historical developments that undermined the components of community and bolstered our cultural infatuation with the individual. In this section of the book, the reader will see that rural history might have been far different and that the "unsettling" of the countryside represents an American tragedy perpetrated by urban commercialist interests under the guise of a meaningless shibboleth called "progress." Chapters 7–9, in Part Three, attempt to point a way toward the simultaneous renewal of rural schools and communities. This part of the book is about as "hands-on" as I could make it. I hope that it paints a realistic portrait of the peaks and valleys that come with this work.

All three parts of the book were written as an attempt to provide the deep-level understanding required to elevate this work from the mere pursuit of a good idea to a moral imperative in one's life. With this in mind I felt obliged to push quite far into historical and philosophical discussion, knowing all the while that given our cultural propensity to disdain such discussion as useless academic banter, I ran the risk of losing readers. Be that as it may, I think that the book, as it is structured, has much to offer those who are willing to work their way through a world of ideas—ideas that have brought about the circumstances that currently define rural lives and livelihoods as well as ideas that may produce different circumstances.

One thing more. Separating the world of rural education—what it is and what it might be—from the realities that have produced rural life and rural living seems to me like a bad idea. For a century, talk of improving rural schools drove thousands of these schools right out of existence. This circumstance stands as the classic example of the consequences of separating discussions about rural schools from their larger contexts. If the casual reader wonders why the ancient Greeks and Romans emerge in a book about rural schools, the careful reader will note that discussion of the Greeks and Romans demonstrates that there have been points in human history when people were motivated by far different things than those that, at least according to most economists, motivate us now. If we are to have any leverage over the critic who rails that the relentless pursuit of profit is unchangeable "human nature," knowledge of human aspirations in other eras comes in quite handy.

I am told that the German philosopher Friedrich Nietzsche once warned an audience, "Read me slowly, I'm dangerous." Although I would not make the same claim, I should warn the reader that the first chapter, "Intradependence," is in some ways, I suppose, the most difficult and may require a slow reading. There is much prerequisite groundwork packed into it, and it therefore probably requires the greatest amount of intellectual flexibility on the part of the reader. Once through it, the reader should find that the rest of the volume becomes more accessible.

Part One

The Creation of Community
from a Historical Perspective

1

Intradependence

I work to renew a ruined place that no life be hostage of my comfort.
—*Wendell Berry, 1974*

The movement toward greater environmental awareness since the 1960s has accomplished a number of things, not the least of which has been more widespread recognition of our dependence on nature. The word "dependence," according to *Webster's New Collegiate Dictionary*, means "to exist by virtue of necessary relations." For a time in this country, we prided ourselves on our *in*dependence from everything, including nature. We glorified the "rugged individualist" who needed nothing and no one. During the nineteenth century, we revered the image of the self-sustaining yeoman farmer. In myth, if not in reality, he personified independence. During the twentieth century, however, we began to speak of "interdependence," or existence by virtue of reciprocal relations. This term seemed to capture the modern economic scene in a way that independence did not. Still, although interdependence speaks of people doing things for each other, it does not completely capture the idea of nature as a player in necessary relations. "Intradependence," however, does. Intradependence means "to exist by virtue of necessary relations *within a place.*"

Throughout most of human history, people lived their lives in a given locality and were highly dependent on the place itself and on those others with whom the place was shared. It has only been since the seventeenth century or so that intradependence of this sort has eroded and people have begun to think of themselves as individuals unencumbered by the constraints of nature or community. "Freedom" was the term we used to describe our unencumbered lives. Prior to this time, the definition of freedom was not so easily divorced from the entanglement of mutual obligations.

Classical Greece presents a fair example of intradependent living. The Greeks lived in a community-oriented world where status was tied to obligations well met. Although the Greeks were far from perfect, they spent a great deal of time and effort discussing the issue of freedom and its relationship to other grand ideas, such as dignity, rationality, and democracy. Operationalizing these ideas in terms of political, economic, and educational policy, as the Greeks did, has come to be known as "classical liberalism." It is important not to confuse this term with the word "liberal" as it is used by the popular media in the 1990s. Strictly speaking, to the degree that we create and execute public policy guided by the dictates of freedom, dignity, rationality, and democracy, we operate in a liberal system. However, use of the term "liberal" throughout this book is a reference to this larger social and political system and not to the ill-fitting contemporary use of the term.

Whereas classical liberals tended to think about freedom, dignity, rationality, and democracy in the context of a community, modern liberals, from the seventeenth century onward, have tended to think about these ideas in terms of what they mean for individuals as independent beings. For example, the Greeks often experimented with a kind of hands-on political obligation on the part of citizens, but modern liberals have preferred the idea of citizens merely choosing representatives. Whereas the Greeks worked at nurturing local economies built around key cities, modern liberals have worked to advance one large, national economy. And whereas education for the Greeks (of the Socratic tradition) tended to revolve around concerted study of ideas like truth, beauty, and justice and how these ideas might advance the quality of community life, education for modern liberals has centered around the preparation of individuals for the economic market. It doesn't take much reflection to recognize which of these ideas are most familiar. Indeed, modern liberal ideas seem so natural to us that it is difficult to see how circumstances might be different.

But things might have been far different. We might have started, for instance, with a definition of individuals as beings dependent on many kinds of relations, including those germane to the place in which they live. From this we might have concluded that the community is the basic human entity, and this would have prompted policy that better served community ends. Had we done this, our political, economic, and educational structures would have been significantly different from those we now know.

We can again turn to the classical Greek experience for an example. For the Greeks, freedom was the outgrowth of human dignity, something to be achieved through the exercise of rational power directed toward the betterment of the "polis," the Greek city-state. Individuals, as far as the Greeks were concerned, were first and foremost members of a community. A person's livelihood was assessed by considering the productive contribution it made to the life of the community. Although productive labor was highly valued, commercial enterprises like trading and banking were seen as parasitic and were considered to be beneath the dignity of citizens.

In a remarkably unmodern way, the classical Greeks lived their lives in the service of their community rather than in the service of their own individual wishes and desires. We will see that in the eighteenth century, modern liberals reversed this mindset and advanced the notion that one could best serve the community merely by pursuing one's own wishes and desires. Whereas the Greeks sought to replicate a kind of harmony in the universe, we have focused on manipulating the earth to our own ends. The Greeks believed there was one best way to live a life, whereas we have maintained that we must each march to our own drummer. The Greeks were so oriented toward community life that they simply did not have a word for "self" as we have since come to define it.

At this point the reader may well be asking "Why is it important to examine Greek thought?" The answer is that it is useful to understand that we borrowed heavily from Greek thinking about rationality, freedom, dignity, and democracy and that these concepts undergird our political, economic, and educational thought. But there is still one more crucial lesson embedded in the Greek experience that speaks directly to questions about the viability of rural communities and rural education. The Greeks demonstrated that it is possible to create a liberal system that is *communally oriented*. Steeped as we are within another worldview—an individually oriented one—it is often difficult to imagine that things might be done in a different way. The Greeks help us to see that human beings can in fact be motivated by something other than material accumulation, that something other than profit can drive an economy, that something other than occupational choice can direct one's education, and that political decisionmaking is the privilege and responsibility of all, not just of those who successfully run for office. The Greek worldview was external; that is, it looked out to the community in an effort to establish a kind of order or harmony. People looked at the community and its needs to find an individual "fit"—the communal role that an individual's life might occupy.

The contrast in worldviews provided by the Greeks is a useful concept. They measured the quality of their lives by the extent of their contributions to the community. Our outlook, however, measures the quality of lives according to what people can accumulate and proclaim as their own. One of the arguments of this book is that strengthening rural schools can help move us back in the direction of a community-oriented worldview.

In order to accomplish this, we need to recognize how very deeply embedded our modern worldview is. How did we move from classical to modern liberalism? How did the outlook change from external to internal? There is no simple answer, for the evolution took place over many centuries. The inward turn, however, is probably most directly attributable to St. Augustine, the Roman Catholic bishop who oversaw the demise of the classical world and the establishment of the feudal world. It was a subtle turn, not a dramatic one, and it was driven by the new idea that what was important about human life was not the relationship one created with the community, but rather the relationship one created with God. An individual needed to turn inward, to be introspective in order to assess the status of this relationship. Free will, according to St. Augustine, gave humans a great deal to inspect through introspection. "How did I handle the situation that came up today? Did I do it in a manner that was pleasing to God?" These are the kinds of questions that slowly turned an individual's attention inward. As the historian Thomas Cahill has pointed out, it was with St. Augustine that the world first witnessed heavy reference to the self, as manifested through the extensive use of the pronoun "I."[1] The end result of a new emphasis on the *individual's* relationship with God was not the enhancement of community on earth, nor was it individual enhancement in the form of material accumulation on earth; it was, rather, individual salvation in heaven.

If this is the worldview and if these are the questions, one can see that the concern with the human ability to exercise rational power becomes significantly less important. And once again, this spills over into various arenas. It reopens the door to autocratic power, and it diminishes the propensity to emphasize the need for mass schooling. The feudal age witnessed both these effects. But life during these centuries remained very communally oriented. For one thing, even though the goal was individual salvation, the only way to get there was through the prescriptions and proscriptions of the church, a kind of community. Furthermore, as we shall see, the life of the medieval peasant was defined by intradependence; that is, it revolved around care and concern for the viability of shared places, something that demanded a communal outlook. In many ways the medieval world remained strongly communally oriented despite the fact that, with St. Augustine, a significant corner had been turned, opening a door to a modern, individually oriented outlook.[2]

The turn became more dramatic during the sixteenth-century Reformation. From the time of St. Augustine, the Catholic Church remained a pivotal focal point in medieval life, though it had been severely divided and tested from time to time. The collapse of its near-complete religious control over western Europe is most often attributed to two individuals, John Calvin and Martin Luther. Both of them rejected certain elements of the Catholic faith, but their theology is not what concerns us here. Rather, it was their promotion of the idea that humans had a choice in the matter of religion that caused the upheaval, for the work of Calvin and Luther handed this possibility to the Western world (though neither of these reformers would have made this one of their goals). John Rawls has argued that the Reformation, by introducing the concept of autonomy into what it means to be human, marks the very beginning of modern liberalism.[3] What was essential about the Reformation was not that it cut into the power of the Catholic Church but that it gave people the opportunity to make choices. Individual autonomy, combined with Augustinian introspection, laid the foundation for an individual orientation to life that would take shape in the seventeenth century and would begin to touch the lives of millions during the eighteenth.

For hundreds of years the Catholic Church remained the authoritative source of knowledge about the world. The sixteenth-century Reformation called this tradition into serious question. Although it is true that the various Protestant groups tried to set up their own kinds of ecclesiastical authority, one can make the argument that a kind of "Pandora's box" was opened by the reformers and that the near-totally religious nature of the dominant way of looking at the world was torn apart.

Skeptics asked where they might go for answers about the world if the church did not possess ultimate authority on such questions. The immediate post-Reformation period is therefore often labeled the "Renaissance," or the period of the rebirth of inquiry, because more and more intellectuals, at least, turned to themselves for answers. And they were bolstered in their conviction to search for answers by revisiting the ancient Greek philosophers. They appropriated the Greek idea that humans have unlimited rational power, and they gave it a new twist. Instead of harnessing this power in the service of community, instead of being the passive recipients of a world order divined by God, humans could utilize their rational power for themselves by manipulating nature in such a way as to order the world to suit themselves.

The French mathematician and philosopher René Descartes was probably the most influential figure in shaping the increasingly individually oriented worldview. He took the Greek emphasis on human rationality as the measure of the individual's gift to the community and transformed it into the measure of a person's humanness. The quality of an individual life was determined by the rational power that a person could generate. For Descartes, the distinctive human attribute was simply thought, and we can see this in his now-famous phrase, "I think, therefore I am."[4]

One can readily see that renewing this Greek emphasis on rationality might not please church authorities. In fact, Descartes' life was filled with worry that he, too, like his contemporary Galileo, might be called before church authorities. In a curious way, however, the Cartesian emphasis on rationality meshed well with the introspective turn the notion of selfhood had taken after St. Augustine. Humankind,[5] given its ability to think about the world, could thereby equip itself with the ability to act upon the world. Here, I believe the words of Descartes himself are instructive:

> It is possible to reach knowledge that will be of much utility in this life; and that instead of speculative philosophy [about the divine order] now taught in schools we can find a practical one, by which knowing the nature and behavior of fire, water, air, stars, the heavens, and all other bodies which surround us, as well as we now understand the skills of our workers, we can employ these entities for all the purposes for which they are suited, and so make ourselves the masters and possessors of nature.[6]

Francis Bacon, Descartes' contemporary and colleague in England, believed that humans possessed the ability to render nature "our slave."

We can see that the seventeenth century added a couple of key ideas to the evolution of a modern worldview. Selfhood remained and in fact became increasingly defined by its introspective nature. Seventeenth-century thinkers like Descartes and Bacon were convinced that one determined who one was through inward searching and reflection. In addition, autonomy, or the power to make choices, was also a crucial contributor to selfhood. Both searching and reflection could be well pursued through the application of rational power. And with this power came the wherewithal to transform the world in order to achieve one's ends or desires.

It is now possible to list the building blocks of modern liberalism—introspection, autonomy, rationality, and a capacity for singular action on the world—and to see how they became the basis for a fundamental shift from a communally oriented to an individually oriented worldview. This individual orientation will become clearer if we look briefly at how these modern liberal tenets shake out in political, economic, and educational thought. In the realm of politics, for instance, modern liberals saw clearly what the Greeks had seen centuries earlier: that the capacity for rationality imbued humans with a certain dignity, a dignity that meant nothing without a commitment to human freedom. If you play out this thinking still further, you can see that there is no room for monarchical or totalitarian power in this worldview. But how, then, could free, autonomous, singularly acting individuals govern themselves? This was the question confronted by eighteenth-century Enlightenment philosophers, and their answer was something called "contract theory."

Keep in mind that fulfillment for modern liberals was tied up with the ability of an individual to pursue personal material desires. What was needed was a government that would not interfere in this process (thus the popular Enlightenment phrase "laissez faire"). But singularly acting individuals will inevitably run into other singularly acting individuals, and what's to keep one such person from interfering with another? To ensure there would be order in an individually oriented world, Enlightenment philosophers argued that autonomous, free, rational individuals needed to enter into a contract with one another to create a government that would be the great arbiter and peacekeeper in society (government was the entity charged with maintaining "domestic tranquillity," to use another eighteenth-century phrase). The function of government was to create a peaceful, harmonious society by harnessing the ostensible mutual benefit derived from individuals busily pursuing their own interests.

Next, in the economic realm, people were not to be burdened with producing a good society but rather were to be free to accumulate whatever wealth they could acquire. According to Adam Smith, author of two famous eighteenth-century economic treatises, *The Theory of Moral Sentiments* and *The Wealth of Nations*, an "invisible hand" would orchestrate the affairs of the marketplace and thereby produce the good society. Individuals would contribute to societal well-being simply by vigorously pursuing their own ends. Concern for producing either a kind of natural harmony or virtuous citizens who would shoulder the burden of meeting community needs was pushed aside in order to legitimate the manipulation of nature in the interest of profit. And if this ushered in forces that were "red in tooth and claw," as Alfred Lord Tennyson later described them, one should not be too quick to condemn the results. Adam Smith carefully explained that when our interpretation of human motives and God's purposes comes into play, we often "imagine that to be the wisdom of man, which is in reality the wisdom of God."[7] In other words, God was creating the world through the expression of our material desires. Community traditions that impeded economic expansion, therefore, were increasingly seen as outdated, backward, or worse.[8]

Last, in the educational realm, the eighteenth century witnessed a great leap forward in the amount of formal schooling available in western Europe and the United States. By the end of the nineteenth century, free public schooling (though very often segregated by race) was almost universally available, at least in the United States. A worldview that rests heavily on human rational power cannot help but suggest that schooling ought to be widespread, and indeed, many of our founding fathers felt that a system of free schools ought to be one of the first orders of business in the various colonies-turned-states. Thomas Jefferson, for instance, tried (unsuccessfully) three times to get Virginia to pass a free-school bill.

It was in England, however, that the educational agenda for the emerging industrial state first began to take shape. Indeed, Adam Smith distinguished himself as one of England's first advocates of compulsory state-directed schooling. But whereas Smith was concerned with the creation of a common culture that would grease the skids for a smoothly functioning market economy, his early nineteenth-century followers, most notably the utilitari-

ans James Mill and Jeremy Bentham, were much more interested in schooling as enculturation into appropriately competitive motives. Mill and
Bentham were advocates of the "monitorial" system, a schooling practice
created by Joseph Lancaster that structured in a competition for the head
of the class. In short, the modern liberalism that emerged from the seventeenth century culminated in an ethos that suggested schooling for all but,
when finally realized, emerged as a mode of schooling steadfastly in the service of larger political and economic concerns.[9]

*   *   *

We now have at least a minimal outline or framework for understanding
how the external worldview of classical liberals was gradually transformed
into the internal worldview of modern liberals. It was modern, individually
oriented thinking about dignity, freedom, rationality, and democracy that
turned the feudal world on its head. Of course, there were other dynamics
involved that one could throw into the mix. There was a growing commer-
cialism that coincided with the evolution of the modern outlook and resulted in an event called the "industrial revolution." The demise of medieval usury laws was an important contribution to this process. Since the
time of Thomas Aquinas in the thirteenth century, the lending of money at
interest had been expressly forbidden (though this stricture was routinely
ignored) throughout most of Europe. Laws such as this were designed to
prevent people from using one another for their own private gain. Because
for a number of centuries there had been no ready lending source to which
individuals might go to meet some exigency or other, communities developed an ethos that included prompt attention and care for the particular
needs of community members. Although this characteristic is centuries old,
it lingers in parts of rural America today. For example, if a farmer suffers
from an accident or illness and is temporarily out of commission, neighbors
will frequently pitch in with the help needed to maintain the man's farm
until he is back on his feet. For all practical purposes, this phenomenon
does not exist in urban and suburban America. The abolition of usury laws
and the establishment of insurance houses slowly eroded the crucial element
of mutual obligation that historically undergirded and, in some ways, defined the notion of human community.

But if you lived in the eighteenth century and you took advantage of
changing circumstances to make your living, the demise of a communal orientation was something that couldn't happen soon enough. Say you developed your own shipping business in Liverpool, England. Everything you
had ever owned was tied up in your fleet of ships. What would happen if
the king or Parliament (made up of an agricultural aristocracy)—neither
representing your interests—decided arbitrarily to close the port of Liver-

pool? If you were in such a situation you would want to run with the idea of man's rationality, autonomy, dignity, and freedom as far as it would take you. Or if you lived in a distant colony like Virginia and you were ceaselessly taxed without your consent, you might want to run with these ideas as well. And this is precisely what happened.

These developments created a powerful cultural trajectory toward an individual orientation in public policy, but by no means was that the only viable trajectory that might have been chosen. The fact is that ideas such as economics based on the maximization of profit, leadership provided by those who ostensibly have the most merit, or education as a profoundly individual undertaking are not based on any divine law or law of nature (such as "human nature"). They are social constructions that have proved enduring for a number of centuries for reasons that we have discussed, but they will not continue to direct the future of the world indefinitely.

The reason they won't, or so this book will argue, is that the modern liberal worldview is far too structurally inattentive to the welfare of communities. One needs only to drive through East St. Louis and into the small towns of Illinois to see that both types of communities are dying. They represent two different American tragedies, and although our concern is with the demise of the latter type, the same forces have been and are still destroying both. The ascendancy of the modern liberal worldview during the seventeenth century has slowly eroded the communal dimensions of living to the point that we no longer know quite what they are or what they were; and indeed, it is common to hear individuals today claim that they are not sure there ever really was such a thing as a communal orientation to life. This is a profoundly ahistorical assessment, of course, but history has never been a cultural favorite of Americans (there are reasons for this, which we will discuss in Chapters 2 and 3). Henry Ford, for example, thought history was "bunk."

When we care to look, however, history tells us a good deal about humans and their dependence on place. Historian Victor V. Magagna, for example, has contended that there was an "intimate connection between territory and community" that historically defined rural lives and livelihoods. In the past, "to belong to a rural community was to belong to a specific place."[10] Further, this intradependence cut across national boundaries. It has been noted by historians and anthropologists in almost every corner of the earth.

Intradependence speaks of dependence within a place, dependence on the land and dependence on the good will and wisdom of the people with whom the land is shared.[11] The greater the intradependence, the greater the sense of community. Modern suburban living, for example, is often considered devoid of communal dimensions.[12] In that environment, neither the place nor the people depend much upon each other. Although residents of suburban neighborhoods sometimes share rides to work, such neighborhoods frequently have no political or economic space within which neighbors might come together. All of this suggests what I take to be a workable definition of community: a place marked by intradependence.

This is lost in large parts of the United States for a variety of reasons. I will come back to this point later when I discuss the identifiable common denominator that undergirds the various forces that have diminished intradependence in a place. First, however, I believe it is helpful to look at how intradependence evolved alongside modern forces after the demise of the classical world.

*   *   *

Although it is true that after the fall of Rome very uneven power relations marked feudal society, peasant farmers at times achieved surprising degrees of independence from their lords. Gaining this independence allowed them to achieve remarkable degrees of intradependence in their place, in other words, to achieve enduring, productive communities. From the eleventh to the thirteenth centuries in western Europe small agricultural communities were remarkably stable. This stability was accomplished by individuals with the sense and wisdom necessary to attend to a place. Soil fertility was maintained and was indeed improved over the centuries through their practice of integrated crop-livestock agriculture. The extent of small family holdings was defined according to the capacity of the holding to produce an appropriate balance between the number of acres and the number of animals available to adequately manure the land. Forests provided fuel, and clearings were used for grazing. Both were cared for communally by the peasant neighborhood. A half-century ago, G. H. Sabine aptly described the intradependent nature of the medieval peasant community:

> The village and neighborhood groups in which men lived and worked were relatively permanent or only slowly changing, and they were relatively small. By long habituation men understood their positions in them. In them they had status and enjoyed respect. The range of opportunity was small, but expectations and prospects were relatively secure at least so far as they depended upon the social structure; the chances and mischances of life that comes from living in an uncertain world were for the most part not the effect of conditions within the social group. Authority operated within relations of rank that were largely accepted as a matter of course. The values of good workmanship, of neighborliness, and of honest dealing were carried by codes that were habitual to the group. Within such a group the individual's life stretched out before him from childhood with each step clearly marked, and the place that he was to fill as an adult was easily foreseen. The gains that he could hope to make were there to be seen, the steps toward them were readily comprehensible, and the obliga-

tions that he was expected to assume appeared as the logical consequences of the training he received. By and large men throughout history have found their place in the world of societies of this kind and have developed their sense of moral obligation from the ties that existed within such groups.[13]

Ever since the Enlightenment philosophers set in motion a cultural propensity to ridicule what to them was rural parochialism or downright foolishness, notions of rural backwardness have flourished. The popularity of arguments concerning Enlightenment rationality not only undermined the scholastic concern for realizing the divine order but also put an end to a culture very much defined by superstition, magic, and mystery. The charge of ignorance that went with the condemnation of rural life has proved to be remarkably enduring. In fact, it remains a strong theme in American culture today. As evidence, recall the ignorant brothers Larry, Daryl, and Daryl from the popular TV sitcom *The Bob Newhart Show*, or consider *The Beverly Hillbillies*. One could even look to classic American literature for the same theme: Recall that the Joads of John Steinbeck's *The Grapes of Wrath* were simple *and illiterate* country people.

This is an important issue and deserves a bit more attention. As anyone who is familiar with rural schooling in this country knows, there are subtle, though widespread, assumptions about the superiority of "town kids" when compared to those who take the bus in from the countryside. The distinction is as old as Aesop's fable about the town mouse who visits his cousin in the country, but it picked up its culturally pervasive status only after the Enlightenment. As with most stereotypes, one can analyze the circumstances responsible for their diffusion within a culture. One such circumstance that came in for heavy criticism by Enlightenment thinkers was the practice of putting animals on trial. The divine order, that is, God's creation, was something taken very seriously throughout the Middle Ages. One didn't wantonly destroy, say, beetles, despite the fact that they may have been jeopardizing a harvest. In such a case, the matter was brought before ecclesiastical courts, learned counsel was appointed to defend the beetles, and more often than not, the rights of the pests were upheld. They were a part of the natural order—God's natural order—and as such, they had a right to exist. From our vantage point, the whole affair seems silly. And it might seem sillier. Consider a sixteenth-century description of the case of the rats in the Autun Diocese:

> Although the rats had been summoned [to court] in due form, he [the defense attorney representing the rats] managed to obtain that his clients be again served a writ by the priest of each parish, given, he said, that since the cause concerned all rats, all rats should be notified. Having won this point, he endeavored to show that they had not been given enough time; that it was nec-

essary to take into account not only the distances to be traveled, but the difficulty of the journey, a difficulty made all the greater by the fact that cats were on the alert, present in every alleyway.[14]

Such practices seem so culturally foreign because the Enlightenment generation spread the idea that humankind, equipped with rational power, was all that mattered. Recall that Francis Bacon argued that nature was to become "our slave."

In speaking of native cultures, Philip Slater has made a crucial point about the notion of rural backwardness that at the same time helps to clarify what I mean by the notion of intradependence:

All the errors and follies of magic, religion, and mystical traditions are outweighed by one great wisdom they contain—the awareness of humanity's organic embeddedness in a complex natural system. And all the brilliant, sophisticated insights of Western rationalism are set at naught by the egregious delusion on which they rest—that of human autarchy.[15]

Robert Redfield has made almost the same point in reference to the kind of peasant cultures we are considering here. According to Redfield, peasant cultures possessed "an intense attachment to native soil; a reverent disposition toward habitat and ancestral ways; a restraint on individual self-seeking in favor of family and community; a certain suspiciousness, mixed with appreciation of town life; a sober and earthly ethic."[16]

Among peasant cultures, there was a mutual dependence between the place and those who shared it. This intradependence was not easily managed, but the difficulty added meaning to peasant lives. It resulted in the maintenance of community, for maintaining a balance in an ecology dominated by plow agriculture, and doing it for centuries, required the creation of norms and sanctions. Those who lived in a given neighborhood were responsible to one another for the maintenance and care of the place. Often this required the selection of an official or officials to watch over the condition of the common grazing lands, the wood supply, the water supply, and so forth. Peasant self-regulation of western European ecosystems in, say, the thirteenth century, represents a high point of intradependence. The health of the ecosystem was maintained and improved over centuries of utilization via the careful attention of individuals committed to their place.

But something needs to be said here about technology. For instance, the spinning wheel was invented in the twelfth century and was not substantially improved until the eighteenth. Why? This is a significant question because residents in rural America today often sentimentally cherish the spinning wheel that belonged to great-grandmother, used as late as the first decades of this century. The spinning wheel betrays our peasant origins, and coming to grips with why it continued to be used in this century pretty much unchanged from its twelfth-century form helps us understand something of the power of cultural memory and tradition.[17]

The orientation of the peasant was to the past, and this, as alluded to earlier, frequently led to accusations of "backwardness," or as Karl Marx once put it, "rural idiocy." These charges are unfair and unsophisticated. Peasants were astute students of history, and they used it as a filter to process the myriad of changes that confronted their lives daily: changes in the weather, changes in the earth's ability to produce, changes in livestock health, changes in the condition of outbuildings, changes in the costs of production, changes in the watershed, and hundreds of other seemingly minute details, such as the loss of a few feathers on a hen. The peasant had to attend to it all because the margin for error was minuscule. A peasant's life cut close to the bone. Peasants therefore reacted to changes according to what had produced survival in the past, for this was the goal of peasants; moving up, or jumping on the bandwagon of "progress," as the concept came to be sold to them, was anathema. Progress held no attraction for peasants because they could clearly see what is enormously difficult for us to understand: Defining progress as some invisible hand that drives the market as it drives history is to take whatever control one has over one's life and throw it into the wind, which means, ultimately, into the hands of someone all too willing to use it for personal gain.

Undue preoccupation with the future, from the medieval peasant perspective, unnecessarily put the present at hazard. It was not that peasants ignorantly turned their backs on innovation; it was that innovation came with no guarantee of success. When survival is the game plan, a propensity for innovation is not the ideal characteristic one seeks in a neighbor. Plow agriculture is so invasive that doing it while achieving a kind of natural equilibrium, as European peasants were able to do for centuries, left little room at the margins for experimentation.

Peasants had two other concerns about progress, however. And here we must reinsert the lives of the lords into the medieval peasant community. Some of the labors involved in the farming life are extremely arduous. Grinding grain represents a good example. The difficulty obviously led to new ideas that might make the job easier. With the resources necessary to construct water-powered grinding mills, lords were able to create another avenue for deriving wealth from the lives of peasants: They would grind peasant grain for a fee. But faced with another drain on their already meager resources, peasants often constructed small hand-powered mills to operate on their own. Lords frequently reacted by passing legislation forbidding the operation of hand mills. They sometimes forcibly entered peasant homes to smash them. And this was not an isolated phenomenon. It was an ongoing struggle between the two groups that lasted for centuries, in

England as well as in most other European countries.[18] In fact, the historical antagonism between farmers and millers dates back to this time period. This leads to the second concern: The benefits of new technology for the peasants themselves were seldom clear. In the case of milling technology, peasant resistance was due to careful economic calculation. Thus, there were two powerful reasons for peasants to be suspicious of new technology: the economic price tag and the probable accompaniment of unfavorable power dynamics.

The high degree of intradependence in the medieval peasant community was achieved through careful attention to the earth itself, to the past, and to the economics of survival. Many innovations brought risk as well as the potential for further exploitation from the lords. Others brought less risk and were quickly embraced. The considerations that went into accepting or rejecting technological innovations will be developed more fully in later chapters because although these issues have taken on modern contours, the tensions they produced have persisted in the countryside for centuries. But first I would like to bring this discussion a little closer to home by taking a look at a few circumstances in late eighteenth- and early nineteenth-century New England.

*   *   *

The traditional interpretation of early American history suggests that we were burdened by no peasant traditions, that cheap land was available to almost everyone, and that colonial and early American farmers were smitten by the individualist liberal impulse of the age. The community be damned; American farmers would go it alone. They often chose to live out on their farms, away from neighbors. They produced primarily for profit, and they looked for markets wherever they might be found. If profits were too low or they experienced a lack of opportunity, they went west to start again. No sitting around complaining about how tough things were—the American farmer used the West to vent that peculiarly Anglo propensity for entrepreneurialism.

Although this interpretation continues to be a part of the way we think of ourselves as a country, the discipline of history has all but left it behind. To begin with, the suppositions that there were no peasantlike circumstances here and that there was available land for all simply do not stand up to close historical inspection. As early as the mid-seventeenth century, tenancy rates in some parts of New England were higher than 30 percent. Certainly this was the case for all of New England by the mid-eighteenth century, and in some locations the percentage was a great deal higher. As historian James Henretta put it, "There was never sufficient cleared or improved property, or livestock, or farm equipment, or adequate housing to permit most young men and women to own a farm."[19] A large percentage of young men in eighteenth-century New England were forced to rent land for extended periods before land ownership might become a reality. One reason for this, of course, is that a very small percentage of the population came to own so much. John Pynchon of Springfield, Massachusetts, presents a good example. During the latter half of the seventeenth century, Pynchon came to own the town's only general store as well as all of its sawmills and grain mills. Additionally, he owned approximately 2,000 acres of land. As late as 1685, 113 of the town's 120 adult male residents rented land or housing from Pynchon at some point in their lives. More than one historian has compared these circumstances to the feudal conditions of Europe.[20]

Therefore, it is not precisely true that peasant conditions did not exist and that cheap land was available for all. But it is the last supposition of the traditional interpretation—that Americans were smitten by an individualist liberal impulse—that functions as the greatest inhibitor in understanding the rural history of this country. For this claim, too, it turns out, is erroneous. Although it is true that American farm families tended to live apart from one another on their own land, this in no way indicates a rejection of communal values or a communal orientation. In fact, the evidence is quite clear on this. New England farmers tended to settle very near to those with whom they had been neighbors back in England.[21] This pattern carried over into the middle colonies and beyond into the interior. Dutch settlers congregated in Dutch neighborhoods, and a similar pattern was true for German settlers, Quakers, Seventh-Day Adventists, and other religious or ethnic groups. For example, after the Second Awakening, various Pietist groups tended to cluster together whenever possible. Historians have pointed out that this desire to live among like individuals extended into the world of economics. That is, whenever possible, German settlers tried to do business with German merchants, and Dutch settlers did business with Dutch merchants. As Henretta noted, "the felt need to maintain a linguistic or religious identity was as important a consideration as the fertility of the soil or the price of the land in determining where a family would settle. The 'calculus of advantage' for these men and women was not mere pecuniary gain, but encompassed a much wider range of social and cultural goals."[22]

Something of the feudal mindset indeed carried over into this country. For one thing, early American agriculture was dominated by subsistence operations. Only 25 percent of the total agricultural produce in the northern states, as late as 1820, ended up in either foreign or domestic markets. Seventy-five percent was used or consumed by those who produced it.[23] Thus, survival was the name of the game. As noted earlier, the economics of survival suggest an altogether different set of assumptions about the world from those suggested by the economics of profit. In the world of survival agriculture, the help and cooperation that comes with responsibly sharing communal burdens is as good as insurance or money in the bank. In the world of profit agriculture, a neighbor bars the way to others' expansion and threatens to reduce the going market price for produce. Furthermore, time spent in the service of the community is simply lost time that cuts away at the maximization of production.

Because early American agriculture was primarily a subsistence affair, one can see the sense in having a strong communal orientation. But this orientation suggested itself with the weight of many centuries' worth of accumulated agricultural wisdom and practice. The collective memory of the Western agricultural community proved to be very enduring. Although it is vanishing today, at the end of the twentieth century, it is not yet gone. Thus, we may now continue to chronicle this tradition through the nineteenth- and, finally, the twentieth-century Midwest.

*   *   *

It should be borne in mind that the intention of this chapter is to trace the emphasis on a communally derived intradependence in agricultural neighborhoods. Shifting from seventeenth- and eighteenth-century New England to the nineteenth- and later twentieth-century Midwest allows us to keep an eye on a growing force—Enlightenment-style procedural liberalism—that would continually chip away at the communal underpinnings of agrarian communities. Getting this into focus will require a short digression into political, economic, and educational arenas.

In New England, feudal-like conditions continued to legitimate an agriculture of survival, of subsistence, but how did circumstances play out in the interior (particularly in the Midwest[24])? The peopling of the Plains States took place within a new ideological milieu. Effecting our separation from Britain required a wholehearted embrace of liberal thinking. "All men are created equal," wrote Thomas Jefferson. No individual, in the "state of nature," held dominion over another. He argued further that when a government fails to attend to the needs of the people, it's up to the people to change the government. For this argument to be persuasive, risk taking needed to be legitimized. And so the argument continued: What's to fear from revolution? Humankind (to use contemporary parlance) inevitably progresses. Jefferson was so convinced of this that he once wrote that the "tree of liberty" needs to be "sprinkled with the blood of patriots" every fifty years or so. "Progress" slowly evolved into a cornerstone of liberal thinking. The Anglo migration into the interior was the march of progress itself. This belief, combined with Puritan religious views concerned with the glorification of "God's garden," created an amazingly persuasive argument for ignoring American Indian claims to the land we wanted.

There was actually a great deal of uncertainty regarding how things would shake out in the interior. The ill-fated, infamous "Burr conspiracy," ostensibly an attempt by former United States vice president Aaron Burr to create a new nation in the West, rekindled the fears of many that had been first provoked by unruly westerners in New England itself. There has been speculation that the provisions of the Land Ordinance of 1785, which spoke to attending to the matter of formal education, indicate that the architects of the ordinance thought that education could diminish the likelihood that western farmers might take liberal rhetoric too seriously.

It is interesting to note that if this was indeed the case, their fears were well warranted. In January 1787, about 1,200 farmers in western Massachusetts, led by Daniel Shays, banded together and marched toward Springfield to take over a federal arsenal. They complained about taxes levied in Boston, and their argument was essentially unchanged from the earlier argument about affairs decided in London. Although the Massachusetts militia scattered the Shaysites, merely a month after the rebellion Congress agreed to a general convention to revise the Articles of Confederation. The tide had turned. "We have probably had too good an opinion of human nature in forming our confederation," wrote George Washington. Fellow Virginian James Madison lamented what he took to be an all-too-pervasive "spirit of locality." In two years' time, with Thomas Jefferson, the chief advocate of a locally oriented republic built around an egalitarian agrarian yeomanry, conveniently isolated in Paris as ambassador to France, a highly centralized federal government was created. It seemed to Madison, Washington, and others that the Enlightenment rhetoric so necessary for effecting our separation from Britain was not to be taken too literally now that independence had been won. It would not do, for example, for the masses of white men to have a voice in something so significant as the selection of senators or the selection of the president. It did not take long for those with power in the fledgling republic to discover that the rhetoric that had fueled the revolution, fought to enable men to create their own government, inevitably worked against the possibility of a strong centralized government. As a result, by 1789 the focus of the constitutional convention was not so much on the facilitation of the people's voice as it was on the control of that voice. Madison wrote in *The Federalist Papers*: "The inference to which we are brought is, that the causes of faction cannot be removed, and that relief is only to be sought in the means of controlling its effects."[25] This is, essentially, Madison's logic: Localities will inevitably come into conflict. Therefore, the role of government ought to be that of the great arbiter, the creator and implementer of policy and procedures designed to keep people apart.

Instead of running with a Jeffersonian version of liberal thought, instead of agreeing that (perhaps aided by formal schooling) reasonable people in a free society would elevate the common good over their own interests, Madison hit on a solution that left nothing to chance. As Daniel Kemmis aptly described Madisonian theory, "individuals would pursue their private ends, and the structure of government would balance those pursuits so cleverly that the highest good would emerge without anyone having bothered to will its existence."[26]

In guaranteeing the pursuit of happiness, or the pursuit of property—regardless of what you want to call it—one thing was clear: The absence of "domestic tranquillity" (to use a Madisonian locution) hindered its execution. A proper government possessed the procedural wherewithal to ensure domestic tranquillity. And so the fledgling American republic placed an official blessing on private pursuits, thereby giving its political stamp of approval to the atomistic underpinnings of modern liberal thought.

In economic reckoning, a similar logic was evolving. In 1776 Adam Smith published *The Wealth of Nations,* in which he argued that an "invisible hand" directed an economy toward growth when individuals pursued their own economic ends. Competition in the marketplace was good for everyone because it was the way to maximize the wealth of the nation. The stress was on the development of a competitive national economy. America's second generation of leading intellectuals—men like Daniel Webster and Henry Clay—were intent on orchestrating market-driven economic policies. Once again, unfettered private pursuit was legitimized, and an economic stamp of approval was placed on the competitive underpinnings of modern liberal thought.

Formal education, too, was affected by modern liberal thinking. Agrarian versions of liberal thought, in this country most clearly articulated by Jefferson, always came equipped with a vision for formal schooling.[27] Jefferson believed that the common good needed to be created by people coming together and being committed to making it happen. Education, from Jefferson's perspective, refined the power of reason-based argumentation, and this, he believed, was the greatest guarantee of freedom within the republic. However, Jefferson's Virginia consistently rejected his plans for free schooling. This was an enterprise still tied closely to religious denominationalism. One of the clear outcomes of the Protestant Reformation and the Catholic Counter-Reformation of the sixteenth century was to entrust education at all levels (at least informally) to the church. Rural dwellers in particular proved to be very reticent to give up church-related control over schooling to a secular state office or, perhaps still worse, to a state office controlled by a clergymen from another denomination. By 1836, however, the idea was popular enough so that several states were on the verge of adopting state-level systems. Massachusetts led the way, and it would be a serious oversight not to recognize the fact that Massachusetts was the most urban and industrial of all the states in the union. It was clear that

Jefferson's dreams of a nation of small, freeholding farmers uncluttered by the "mobs of great cities" was simply not going to be realized. In fact, the atomistic and competitive underpinnings of the liberal thinking shaping our nation had its unpleasant side effects, some of which our procedural republic was not prepared to handle. What should be done, for instance, with the gangs of unemployed Irish Catholic youth ("the down-trodden, ignorant, priest-ridden of centuries," according to one contemporary periodical[28]) roaming the streets of Boston? Schools, it was argued, could correct the evils resulting from both the Catholicism and the unemployment. In schools, *individuals* would demonstrate the ability to compete with other individuals; in short, they would be socialized into accepting (while they were in fact legitimating) the prevailing wisdom about democracy, but democracy carried only as far as the selection of reasonable representatives and economic success resulting from superior marketplace savvy. It is important to see that the migration from New England into the interior took place at a time when a kind of competitive individualism was slowly being institutionalized in political, economic, and eventually, educational realms.

Having said this, it might be legitimate to ask: Is it at this point, then, that the traditional interpretation of early American history kicks in? Do the farmers of the interior shed older communal traditions and press ahead as eager entrepreneurs or rugged individualists? Does this explain the high levels of mobility on the plains, the seemingly ceaseless movement of pioneers from one location to another one further west? New historical work on the West (most notably that by Patricia Nelson Limerick and Richard White[29]) suggests that this interpretation, although squaring well with ascendant political, economic, and educational views of contemporary elites, has never been consistent with circumstances surrounding everyday life.

Over the past seventy years, Americans have lost an appreciation for the arduous nature of life before electricity and the internal combustion engine. The initial work required to carve out a farmstead in the wilderness of the Old Northwest (a name given to the region between the Appalachian Mountains and the Mississippi River north of the Ohio River, which includes Ohio, Indiana, Illinois, Michigan, and Wisconsin) almost defies imagination. Raising a log cabin and a barn of sorts, plowing through prairie ground entrenched with years of entwined root systems, clearing trees and grubbing out stumps, preparing food without the benefit of refrigeration, tanning hides or spinning wool to produce needed clothing, and other such chores all consumed an enormous number of work hours, and these were activities that merely permitted the real work of farming to begin. Maintaining a farmstead, whether in nineteenth-century Illinois or twelfth-century France, was a constant routine of around-the-calendar work. The modern division of life into periods marked either by work or by leisure simply did not exist.[30]

This idea will be developed more fully in later chapters, but one can quickly see the ties between it and the communal nature of agrarian villages and neighborhoods. Work evolved into the medium for the enjoyment of one another's company. A "cabin raising" or "barn raising" was a kind of neighborhood celebration. Furthermore, it created a web of interlocking obligation. Neighbors became responsible to and for one another and for the place they shared. Intradependence, in greater or lesser measure, came to define agricultural communities in the Old Northwest.

But the picture was not all rosy. A young man and woman moving to Illinois during the first half of the nineteenth century would find themselves working hard for years before they might expect to produce more than enough to meet their own needs. In contrast, an older couple with grown children, uncles, aunts, and cousins moving en masse to the same neighborhood could easily quadruple the amount of work hours the young couple might muster alone. Although by all accounts neighbors were exceedingly generous with one another and although they vigorously participated in various sorts of "bees" (communal work projects), the kind of age and wealth stratification that came to mark the New England countryside reappeared in the Old Northwest in short order. In fact, most families that moved to the interior were not able to achieve the dream of land ownership in their first, second, or even third location. They worked until it became obvious that they would never generate the funds it would take to make land ownership in that locale a viable possibility. The ceaseless movement west, then, was not so much a trail marked by eager entrepreneurialism as it was a trail marked by dashed hopes and dreams. As John Mack Faragher put it while describing the Sugar Creek neighborhood in Illinois, "a lack of kin as well as a lack of funds, seems to have accounted for their lack of permanence."[31]

There is another dimension to consider briefly here, although this will be taken up again in Chapter 4. The settling of the interior represented a significant social experiment of sorts, one that was largely unprecedented. It was here that the "separation of church and state" first played itself out. The colonies had been dominated by established or quasi-established state churches. Circumstances on the frontier were different. The various denominations had to claim their own converts on the merits of their theology. This created a fierce ecclesiastical battle for souls. The sectarian division of the antebellum Old Northwest was as sharply divisive as at any point in our history.

Churches played a prominent role in the agricultural communities of the Old Northwest. Families tried to cluster near people of similar religious persuasion. The church functioned as a community focal point, and although attention to the care of the place they shared transcended denominational lines (take the communal labor orchestrated to improve local roads as an example), it was similar religious views, after kinship ties, that gave some people first choice of available commodities; and this may have been enough to adversely affect the fate of some settlers. In a world dominated by a barter and exchange economy, some goods are simply not available at any price (for instance, a needed commodity not earmarked for a family member may have been promised to a church member).

It is also worth bearing in mind that the rush of white Anglo-Saxon Protestants into the interior, bolstered by the increasing liberal emphasis on "progress," led to a kind of thoughtlessness regarding how the land was treated. Unlike in Europe, the frontier was seemingly endless. And the kind of concerted, focused attention on its well-being was therefore not a high priority.

* * *

With due appreciation for these caveats that mar an otherwise clear picture of an enviable sort of intradependence, we can push on to chronicle the communal orientation of rural communities into the twentieth century. As the nineteenth century progressed, those settlers unable to secure land elsewhere ended up in the trans-Mississippi West, often filing (after 1862) for the government gift of a free 160 acres. The older areas of the Old Northwest, of course, were already "filled." The newer areas, like the Dakotas, Kansas, Minnesota, and Nebraska, were the states that provided the greatest opportunity to take up land under the Homestead Act.

We should be clear about what was available in these trans-Mississippi states. Much of the region was "short-grass prairie," land that received significantly less rainfall than the states of the Old Northwest. The trans-Mississippi West included vast expanses of timberless land that left hard-pressed settlers very little building material. Many lived for years in not much more than holes in the ground, which they referred to as "soddies" or "sod houses," since they were made from the earth-strewn root systems of the ancient prairie grasses. Such homesteads frequently used the dried manure of buffalo as a kind of winter fuel. It was often a very desperate existence, and it thus attracted only those who had been excluded from land ownership elsewhere: in the Old Northwest or in Europe. This circumstance made the dynamics that characterized trans-Mississippi communities somewhat different from those in the Old Northwest—somewhat more egalitarian, in fact.[32] And this propensity became further entrenched as America's increasingly well-developed commercialist political economy pressed hard on the heels of the initial wave of trans-Mississippi settlers.

Railroads had a tremendous impact on the development of communities and villages in these states. This is evident in the enormous number of towns named after the children of railroad presidents, the hometowns of railroad presidents, the friends of railroad presidents, and so on. This symbolizes, I believe, how far-reaching the commercialist enterprise in America was becoming and how much it was beginning to muddle the intradependent relationship between people and their places. One can see this as well in the amount of townsite speculation that went on in the final twenty years of the nineteenth century. Eager entrepreneurs, anxious to purchase land that would one day become the site of a thriving town, followed the newly laid rail lines. Most were convinced that they could easily quadruple their money in the right set of circumstances.

Unlike the early settlers of the Old Northwest who were initially forced to get along without a well-established banking system, the new farmers of the trans-Mississippi West had readily available credit. It has been estimated, for instance, that in Kansas in the 1880s there was one mortgage for every two people. The optimistic proclamation that "rain follows the plow," a sentiment that convinced banking houses to overextend themselves, proved to be untrue as years of drought in the late 1880s broke farmers and bankers alike. Drawn together by desperate circumstances, trans-Mississippi farmers formed the Farmers Alliance, a democratic organization dedicated to sorting out ways to address the forces behind its members' afflictions. As historian Lawrence Goodwyn described it,[33] the alliance gave farmers space in which to think.

As farmers raised crops to pay their mortgages, they found that railroad companies could charge exorbitant amounts to ship farm produce. If farmers wished to store their grain for sale at a later date, they ended up paying the same railroad company for that service, too. Rail corporations had found it was in their interest to get into the grain elevator business as well as the shipping business. The tension in the relationship between "millers" and farmers, dating back into the Middle Ages, as previously noted, intensified remarkably in the last years of the nineteenth century. There were intermittent charges that the weighing equipment at the elevator was manipulated to the detriment of the farmer. Frequent fires in these establishments, across all the interior states, were often attributed to some recently departed farmer who had lost everything and blamed it on the fact that he had been cheated at the elevator.

What was happening across the country had, as I noted earlier, a peculiar effect on the trans-Mississippi West. The nation was moving to a monetary economy—and a national one, at that. The entrepreneurial impulses that had led to the establishment of rail companies, grain elevators, banking enterprises, insurance houses, townsite speculation, and so forth all had the effect of eroding the communal dimensions of agricultural communities. In a relatively short time, what people were to make of their lives became less and less defined by what they were able to get done by cooperating with those with whom they shared their place on earth and became more and more defined by forces alien to their neighborhood, by forces represented by strangers, by people they did not know and likely never would know. The farmers of the Old Northwest, while in debt as well, were in far less desperate straits. They lived in houses rather than holes in the ground. They had good reason to believe they could expect a decent return on the investment they had put into their farms. The farmers of the trans-Mississippi West had no such luxuries. Life was hard, and they lived with no guarantees that their farms would ever be worth much of anything. And indeed, during the 1920s and 1930s the worst nightmares of many became reality. But the farmers who joined the Farmers Alliance during the 1880s faced a different sort of problem: They looked at the economic circumstances impinging on their lives and saw that their ability to shape their own destiny was slowly disappearing.

The result was the evolution of the Farmers Alliance into a politically active body, or more simply put, the result was the People's Party. Populist farmers were determined to confront head-on the anticommunal dimensions of the increasingly commercialist-oriented nation. They would come together, pool their resources, and create their own elevators, their own creameries, their own lending houses, and their own insurance interests. Countless farmer cooperatives sprang up all across the interior states, and very few went uncontested by the power of already large (mostly railway) corporations. Page through any small-town newspaper of the 1890s and 1900s, and you will likely read about rail company attempts to undercut the cooperatives. For twenty years it was a predictable feature animating small-town life in the Midwest, and in the end, big business won. Although many ostensibly "cooperative" operations still exist, they remain this in name only. The Populists had sought nothing less ambitious than the establishment of what they called a "cooperative commonwealth," and I think their name for it is instructive.

What they were after was the reinsertion of community life as the nation's dominant value, for they had seen, firsthand, the way that individualism eroded any propensity to consider matters democratically. The Populists of the 1890s were remarkably prescient because they realized that they were instigating a last clash between communal and individual values, between an agrarian and an industrial culture, and between a truly democratic and a merely meritocratic political system. But the attempt was smashed by the growing accumulation of corporate power and the ever-growing propensity of American government, with either of two corporation-dominated political parties in power, to facilitate its use. Most of the drama provided by the Populists of the trans-Mississippi West was finished a century ago. In the intervening decades, those communal characteristics traceable back to the Middle Ages slowly eroded to the point that few linger today. In fact, the tide had turned by 1920. Technology, as we saw in the case of the mills constructed by the feudal lords, certainly played a part in this regard. Aided by the development of the internal combustion engine, rural communities started down a slow path of steady decline. The census bureau refers to depopulation in the countryside as "natural decreases," as if the circumstances were an unavoidable act of nature rather than the result of deliberate choices. Most recently, the bureau decided to stop counting farmers, reasoning that there are just too few to bother.

The logic that legitimizes the demise of rural communities is not as persuasive as it is pervasive. We are ceaselessly told that there are so many more people in the world today—people who need to be fed—that the practice of agriculture, therefore, cannot be constrained by attention to communal values. The slow pace of small-farm agriculture would unnecessarily cut production. Besides being untrue,[34] the view is also ironic, since our government has been experimenting with creative ways to cut agricultural production for the last fifty years. But this logic more than makes up for its lack of persuasiveness by the awesome power of the forces that drive it home. The media advertisements, the agribusiness periodicals, and even the nightly news broadcasts convince us that things are the way they are because they have to be this way. This is shallow, of course, but coming to see just how shallow is not particularly easy. In the remainder of the chapter, I will take up the point mentioned earlier, the matter of the identifiable "common denominator" that undergirds the various forces that have diminished intradependence in a place, that is, the communal dimensions of human life. I hope that coming to grips with the rather amorphous nature of this common denominator will make the task easier.

*   *   *

Thomas Jefferson wrote an autobiography at age seventy-two. Looking back at the days before the Revolution, he mused, "during regal government nothing liberal could expect success."[35] By the end of the eighteenth century, the American Revolution had put an end to the monarchical power of George III, and liberalism had become the dominant way of thinking in the United States, the dominant way of looking at the world. Recall that according to modern thinking of the time, the way to discover one's identity was to look inward, to sort through one's wishes and desires in an introspective attempt to find out what it was one wanted to do. An eighteenth-century German philosopher, Johann Herder, argued that an individual possesses a unique identity, something fundamentally different from all other individuals. This idea remains a strong component of the modern liberal worldview, for it conforms to the Augustinian emphasis on inward reflection. In other words, a person can only determine his or her unique identity by searching within.

Add to this introspective propensity the idea that living with dignity requires the right to be autonomous, the freedom to make choices about how to live, and add to this the belief that an individual has the rational power necessary to make the right choices, and you come up with the framework that undergirds our powerful cultural conception of selfhood as something extremely volitional in character. That is, a self has come to be defined as someone who acts upon the world to achieve individual ends and desires. A liberal economy allows one to do this. A liberal government maintains domestic tranquillity by protecting the rights of individuals from unscrupulous activity in the liberal economy. And increasingly, a liberal education, though a clear distortion of its original concern with matters of truth and justice, equips one for success in the liberal economy. The entanglements of community obligation or commitment to the well-being of a place and to those with whom a place is shared play almost no role in this kind of liberal reckoning. Intradependence, therefore, has gradually disappeared over the last few centuries.

Construing life as an individual enterprise, as modern liberal thinking does, necessitates a government based on rights, an economy based on accumulation, and an educational system that reifies the notion that life is an individual enterprise. This is precisely what we have in the United States today. And nowhere in this scheme is the health of communities taken into account. There should be no mystery about the fact that Americans no longer possess a vocabulary for describing community. The communal dimensions of life have been eroding since sometime shortly after our nation was founded. I have argued in this chapter that the greatest amount of intradependence in a place dominated by agriculture[36] probably existed in medieval peasant communities and that such places were marked by cultural practices that were alive and easily identifiable at our nation's founding but are not so today. The common denominator of all types of rural decline has been the evolution of individually oriented liberal thought about life and what makes it worth living. To make this clearer, we will next take a close look at how modern thinking led to ideas and practices that clashed with one prominent characteristic of historically intradependent communities.

2

Cyclic Time

Time has no divisions to mark its passage.
—*Thomas Mann, 1924*

When people talked about rural schools fifty years ago, they were referring to small one-room concerns that dotted the countryside from Maine to
California, even though these institutions had begun to disappear at a fairly
rapid rate by 1945. There was much that was constant from one school to
the next, but they were different from one another in certain ways as well.
I want to begin this chapter by highlighting one subtle difference.

Some of these schools were conveniently located for all district children,
but most were placed in such a way that some students were at a distinct
disadvantage in getting to and from school. Calling class together, therefore, was never something one could predict with "clocklike regularity." A
rainy day may have made the path to school for some children deplorably
muddy, thereby slowing their arrival considerably. A rain-swollen creek
could mean that others had to detour a significant distance in order to get
to school. In fact, any number of weather-related or farm-related exigencies
could keep some students from being at school at what served loosely as the
appointed hour. For example, if a cow strayed into a field of green corn during the night and died from stomach bloat, quick work would be required
of that family to salvage the meat from the dead animal. School for those
children able to help with this task would undoubtedly be put on hold for
a few hours.

At the schoolhouse, the teacher generally put off beginning the school
day until a quorum of students was reached, at which point she would
begin. By 1945 county superintendents were chiding the teachers under

their dominion to put an end to this way of approaching the practice of schooling. Teachers were told to insist on punctuality under all circumstances and to keep precise records of all instances of "tardiness." City schools had begun to operate in this manner decades earlier, and many city-raised superintendents were bent on converting rural schools to these practices as well. In time, teachers complied and began to make it known that inattention to the dictate of punctuality (albeit an arbitrary sort of punctuality) was evidence of a serious character flaw.

This was a subtle sort of institutional intrusion on local culture, and it nicely highlights the theme of this chapter. A quick look at rural schools in the 1990s shows that their practices are governed (and therefore limited or constrained) by the clock in exactly the same way as urban and suburban schools. But this was not always the case. As rural dwellers came to embrace public schooling, something they were not particularly excited about in the first place, they gradually developed schools that complemented the life of the local community.[1] The schools might close for three weeks during potato-digging season, for instance, or they might stay open a month longer than planned because the local taxpayers were willing to support them and because wet weather was going to keep everyone out of the fields anyway. The idea that the calendar or the clock should dictate school practice merely for the sake of the calendar or the clock or merely for the sake of teaching a value called "punctuality" was an argument farmers, generally, could not understand or appreciate.

There is a reason this was so and it was connected to an observation made in Chapter 1—that liberal thinking geared toward the individual inevitably clashed with thinking geared toward the community. As I have tried to demonstrate, to buy into one of these two ways of thinking predisposes a person to a certain outlook in all kinds of arenas. This is why the term "worldview" is often used to describe such systems for thinking as liberalism, fascism, socialism, communism, and so on. Our concern in this chapter is with what the modern liberal worldview did with the concept of time.

We can see from the above discussion that one of the continuities of rural culture lingering in rural communities at least to the mid-point of this century was a conception of time that was fundamentally unlike the conception of time that had already begun to dominate urban industrial life. Industrial time was based on a linear conception, and this clashed with the cyclic conception that had been in place for centuries. This was a development of great consequence, as we shall shortly see. But first, it's necessary to look back to see how the clash began to take shape.

As was the case in Chapter 1, it is entirely possible to go back to the Greeks and Romans to explore their use of such instruments for measuring time as sundials and hourglasses, but it was the development of the mechanical clock that created the significant, far-reaching changes. And this development brings us back to the medieval world once again. If we revisit twelfth-century France, a period of enviable sustained agricultural production, we might take notice of a significant development within the Benedictine monasteries that dotted the countryside then. In their attempt to increase their Christian devotion through better service to God, Benedictine monks repeatedly broke up their day into periods of worship and work. Because they wanted to do everything they did in the most thorough and Christ-pleasing way, the monks began to experiment with mechanical clocks in order to bring precision to the division of hours.

The clock did that. And more. Neil Postman has persuasively demonstrated that using any piece of technology allows one to do certain things better, more efficiently, and so forth, but at the same time it causes one to do other things poorly, less efficiently.[2] The troubling thing about technology is that what it will do well and what it will do poorly is almost unpredictable. This is a side of technology that its proponents often fail to mention. The clock, as an attempt to bring human life closer to God, proved to be a miserable failure. But as a device for manipulating the behavior of human beings (both children and adults), it has proved to have no parallel. Johann Gutenberg's invention of the printing press provides another excellent case in point. He believed he had invented something that would increase the glory and the dominion of the Roman Catholic Church, but what it did was contribute to a religious reformation from which the Catholic Church has not recovered.

The clock never attracted much interest among the peasants of Europe (although the same cannot be said about the growing urban, commercial class). And it is true today that a farmer's work is rarely connected to a clock, just as it was true fifty years ago that farmers could see little sense in recording instances of "tardiness" at the local school. In some ways, today's farmers remain at least partially tuned in to a very ancient conception of time, a circular conception wedded to the rhythms of the seasons and the corresponding wisdom concerning agricultural practice.[3] One scholar refers to this as an "organic and functional periodicity" that is increasingly giving way to a culturally powerful "mechanical periodicity" that manifests itself in schedules, timetables, dismissal bells, stopwatches, alarm clocks, and the like.[4] It is true, however, that as reliance on agribusiness inputs has increased, the importance of clock time has as well. The application of petrochemical fertilizers, for example, requires that work be done with more and more attention to this kind of time. Additionally, heavy investment in large equipment reduces the options of farmers, often forcing them to accomplish one (and only one) task in a given window of time.

The embrace of the clock in the fourteenth-century urban centers of Europe led to a day's division into twenty-four hours and to further refinement of the twelve-month Roman calendar. Prior to this, the length of "hours" depended on the season and the corresponding amount of sunlight that came with it. Plowing, planting, cultivating, and harvesting, along with a myriad of other activities such as wood gathering, shearing, castrating, hoof trimming and shoeing, breaking animals, butchering, soap making, spinning, weaving, candle making, and so on, were all activities governed by the season. They were all traditional skills as well, the competence for which was widespread across rural America well into this century.

For readers to grasp the full significance of a cyclic conception of time, a conception marked by reoccurring cycles of work, I need to introduce one of the ramifications of the embrace of linear industrial time. As mentioned earlier, the introduction of the clock as a piece of technology did nothing quite so well as that it enabled people to manipulate the lives of others. When coupled with the introduction of a money economy (our currently popular phrase "Time is money" makes it easy to see how the clock facilitated such a link), clock-governed time created a distinction between time "spent" (note the economic undertone) at work and time spent living, or at leisure. No such distinction troubled the medieval world. In order to appreciate the cycles that defined time for the peasant, we need to appreciate the fact that they also defined the peasant's life. The dynamic is no different than the one we put in motion today. We cling to a conception of life as something divided into sequential steps: childhood, adolescence, adulthood; or preschool, school, work, and retirement. We have defined life as sequenced steps because we have made time linear. If we can step out of this worldview, it makes it easier to see that peasants saw the world very differently. They viewed their lives—and everything around them—as part of a cycle with no clear beginning or end. Peasants saw themselves as a part of the past with a contribution to make, through their children, to the future. The children, in their turn, rejoined the circle by becoming a part of the past.

Something should be said here about the demanding work that marked the life of the medieval peasant. We have all been raised to look upon new technology as "labor-saving," and the connotation we are supposed to attach to this phrase is that this is unquestionably good. As a consequence, it is culturally difficult for us to appreciate the fact that hard work performed well can in fact be sustaining to the personality. We know enough about the history of the countryside, however, to know that the rhythmic nature of life and work, a rhythm that matched the cyclic conception of time, had a calming psychological effect despite its repetitive nature.

To try to gain some perspective on this you might juxtapose it against the anxiety that accompanies sitting for some kind of standardized test in school. Students work feverishly, all the while dreading those words that come too quickly: "Time is up. Pencils down." Or you might think of the stress that comes with cooking or waiting on customers at a busy restaurant during a noon rush or the stress you experience when the "time-and-motion guy" brings the stopwatch to measure how long it takes you to pass a product down the factory line. There's a fundamental distinction between the work that evolved out of centuries of agriculture and the work that evolved out of what we like to call the "industrial revolution." In the former, time is thought to be in the service of the task at hand. In the latter, the task at hand is in the service of time. In the former, time reappears each day, true to its cyclic nature; in the latter, time is lost, true to its linear nature. It does not take a great deal of deep thinking to see how this circumstance alone, if taken seriously enough, could have negative psychological and cultural consequences.

Just a superficial glance at the twentieth-century industrial West ought to be enough to convince anyone that there are a few cultural flaws that stand in need of some attention. This has been the century of total war, the first century in which there have been no such people as "noncombatants." No age has known death and destruction as we have known it. It has been an age without limits on greed and material accumulation, and just as this has meant the premature death of millions and millions of people, so it has meant widespread death in nature as well. We have done more ecological damage to the planet in this century than has been done in all others combined.

By contrast, cyclic conceptions of time have had a stabilizing effect on culture, at least if we can agree to define culture as the sum of human practices developed in response to a place on earth. Since most anthropologists would have little difficulty with this definition, we will not stop to consider it more deeply. I use the term "stabilize" with respect to the effect of cyclic conceptions of time on culture because such a conception builds in its own logic against overproduction and the unstable conditions that accompany excessive accumulation. In cyclic conceptions of time, "what goes around comes around." If there's an imbalance of what is sowed, there will be an imbalance of what is reaped. If you try to overseed in the interest of a greater harvest, the end result may well be diminished harvests at some later time. Some anthropologists speak of the "ethic of the limited good" among peasants in order to differentiate their outlook from ours—we who ostensibly know better and embrace an "ethic of the *unlimited* good." But this puts us ahead of the story.

To go back just a bit, the fourteenth century, as I mentioned, was the century that embraced the use of the mechanical clock. It was also the century that put an end to several hundred years' worth of increased agricultural production combined with increased soil fertility. It would be stretching things, however, to say that the two developments were tightly connected. Population was increasing rapidly at the start of the fourteenth century, and this, combined with the increased demands for rents, tributes, and tithes coming from the lords, pushed what had been an ecologically sustainable system to the limit. Years of drought beginning about 1315 led to widespread hunger and ultimately to the infamous Black Death, or bubonic plague. The dramatic reduction in Europe's population over the next one hundred years reduced the ecological pressure and allowed patterns of sustainable agricultural production to return.

But years like those in the eleventh and twelfth centuries were never to return. As Europe moved into the sixteenth and seventeenth centuries, some drastic changes were in the works, and they were all at least tangentially connected to our ever-increasing ability to accurately "measure" time. For instance, it was during the seventeenth century that minute hands began to appear on clocks, and it was also during this century that watches became widely available.

I use the phrase "measuring time" because it is one of those phrases that helped to spell the end of the medieval period, the end of feudal organization, the end of a pronounced Christian presence in politics and economics. One measures time not to create some exactitude in a life lived for Christ, as the Benedictines once thought, but in order to know how much to spend for it. We still casually use the phrase "Let's spend some time together," without recognizing the economic relationship it implies. The tremendous expansion of the money economy during the sixteenth and seventeenth centuries, itself spurred on by a frantic European scramble for chunks of the "New World," wedded itself nicely to the notion of linear time.

This juncture, when the money economy caught up to the mechanical clock, represents a moment in history as powerful and portentous as any other throughout history. Its significance lay merely in this: Since money (as John Locke demonstrated so persuasively) eliminates natural restrictions on accumulation (it never spoils), the past is a burden to no one. In other words, since time is not cyclic and because it is linear, one can get on here and get off there. What goes around goes out the door. There is no day of reckoning for upsetting a cyclic balance.

The advent of the money economy meant that individuals, as opposed to neighborhoods and families, became the pivotal economic players. With this development, the wisdom of tradition began to hold less power. There has been an ever-present "ahistoricism" associated with our modern liberal system ever since the linear conception of time emerged in Europe, an ahistoricism perhaps best symbolized by Henry Ford's reference to history as "bunk."

During the seventeenth century, however, the obvious connection between the natural cycle of birth, growth, decline, and death and an understanding of time did not give way easily. To comprehend how seventeenth-century intellectuals could diminish cyclic conceptions of time, one needs to get a feeling for how they were able to demonstrate man's dominion over what was "natural."

There are a number of ways to accomplish this, but I'd like to make an attempt by using the work of one of the seventeenth century's leading figures, Francis Bacon. Bacon (1561–1626) is widely considered to be one of the founders of the "scientific revolution." This revolution, I contend, was driven by both the ramifications of the ability to measure time and the ramifications of an increasingly widespread switch to a money economy. Accurately measuring time increased the power of scientific experimentation tenfold. The growth of the money economy put science steadfastly into the service of industry, commerce, invention, and colonization. Perhaps more than any other seventeenth-century figure, Francis Bacon melded the seemingly opposed ends of cold, objective scientific experimentation and the hot pursuit of ever-greater material accumulation. The delusion that the "pursuit of scientific truth" rested on no metaphysical assumptions, that is, that it was based on no human construction of what constitutes reality, has only recently received widespread criticism. In the seventeenth century, proud scientists needed only to dance around the power of the established church. If Galileo became a little careless in his dance, men like Bacon and Descartes negotiated this step quite nicely. Science, Bacon left no doubt, would enlarge the "bounds of human empire." Scholars before Bacon's time were far more concerned with expanding the bounds of God's empire. The experimentation inherent in the scientific "method," Bacon went on, would render nature "our slave." Descartes, in France, wrote similarly: Humans were destined to become the "masters and possessors of nature."

As these seventeenth-century scientists dug deeper and deeper into the mysteries of nature, they became convinced that the earth was a big machine, a machine that differed from the machines they were fond of creating only in size. They became so convinced that the world was a mechanism governed by laws that they began to proudly boast that the eventual discovery of these "laws" would enable humans to create machines that would do fantastic things. As early as 1609, for example, Johannes Kepler predicted humankind's eventual flight to the moon. He wrote to a friend a few years earlier: "I am much occupied with the investigation of physical causes. My aim is to show that the celestial machine is to be likened not to a divine organism but rather to a clockwork."[5]

Another seventeenth-century English scientist, Sir Isaac Newton, rose to the status of "revealer of natural laws" within his own lifetime. The poet Alexander Pope immortalized Newton's contributions:

Nature and nature's laws lay hid in night;
God said, "Let Newton be," and all was light.

Francis Bacon was sometimes referred to as the "new Moses," the individual who would lead the world to a kind of scientific perfection. In his hands, along with those of many other seventeenth-century scientists, the world was converted to a machine that ran on linear time. And the purpose of a machine, as everyone knew, was to serve humans. This new mechanical view of the world had to unseat an older, highly religious view of the earth as a kind of organism marked by a propensity for natural harmony. This subtle blow to the dogmatic authority of the established Christian churches was followed by a drive during the eighteenth century to separate religion from the political realm altogether. Here, of course, the story becomes a little more familiar, for Americans were among the first to loudly proclaim the "separation of church and state" as something so self-evidently wise that it was akin to a law of nature.

But we must avoid, once again, getting too far ahead of the story. Linear conceptions of time and all the emphasis on instrumental scientific work it advanced, all the mechanistic metaphors it promoted, the way it loaned itself to a money economy, the way it eased the divorce of history as any kind of guide for present action—these things all had to hinge on some kind of certainty, and it was obvious that this certainty was not going to come from the chairs of theology in Europe's great universities. Some manner of proof was required in order to sell these changes, and that proof took the form of mathematical computation as a part of what came to be called "the scientific method."

To this day, nothing is quite so important in the world of science as "method." Use it appropriately and no philosophical argumentation is required. As mentioned earlier, scientists believed they could ignore metaphysics by merely donning the cloak of objectivity, the symbolism of which claims loudly: "There are no value assumptions at work here."

I think it is important to delineate the crucial importance placed on method (Descartes' *Discourse on Method* is still one of the most widely cited books on the subject) only because the method rested heavily upon reducing things to parts. The reductionism of modern science, as it was advanced in the seventeenth century, has colored all subsequent political, economic, and educational thought. Reductionism suggested economic specialization and the accompanying clock-driven breakup of labor tasks, it suggested a system of checks and balances in politics that would make government operate in a machinelike fashion, and it suggested the breakup of knowledge in educational settings into ever-smaller disciplinary realms (or a broad array of unrelated discipline-driven curricula in the schools). It has taken over two hundred years to get to the point where one can question the wisdom of these developments and be taken seriously, for, we must remember, these developments were wrapped in the cloak of objectivity achieved through the faithful application of the value-free scientific method.

I believe it is useful to look at the American countryside as the stage on which the great seventeenth-century science drama unfolded. Reducing the practice of agriculture to fewer and fewer tasks with bigger and bigger machines meant greater and greater levels of dispossession as the nation's history unfolded. This created profound changes in the character and quality of rural communities. As family members left the countryside to join the urban industrial economy, less and less security remained for those who stayed. Whereas family and neighbors had once been the source of security, in their absence money became all the remaining rural dwellers could cling to. And clinging too hard to this source of security, of course, meant that still fewer family members or neighbors were around to count on. In the storytelling that goes on in small agriculturally oriented towns today, there are at least two stories about brothers who fought one another at every turn in the scramble for a secure economic foothold for every story of brothers who worked together and made it. This makes up one of the saddest chapters in the story of the rural Midwest.

The reductionism of science related to agricultural production has left farming so capital-intensive that researchers in this area simply cannot support their own efforts and neither can the universities for whom they ostensibly work. They must be funded by the multinational agribusinesses that, of course, only give money to projects that suit their purposes. Woe to the agricultural researcher who would like to do some work that might have the effect of reducing the farmer's reliance on agribusiness inputs! The enormity of that struggle is reflected by the fact that one has to look long and hard to find such researchers in colleges of agriculture. I have known many professors in that business who cover their uneasiness about the fact that they are not their own masters with the fiercest sort of defensiveness in the face of the slightest hint that agriculture might move in another direction.

The point of this chapter, of course, is to demonstrate the significance of the linear conception of time that evolved with the mechanical clock in contrast to the much older, much less arbitrary, cyclic conception of time. Rural people will often recognize cyclic time as something that lingers, a rural continuity that has endured over the last three centuries despite a powerful cultural trend that has pervasively worked to demolish it. Many rural residents can still feel the impending winter during fall days or the coming of spring in late February in ways that their city cousins cannot. Thoughtful scholars contend that there are organic impulses within humans and that they are rhythmic in nature. Some argue that even the way we think is closely tied to the landscape in which we find ourselves.[6] Rural dwellers often live with an attention to natural rhythms, something that has evolved from close association with the earth and, in particular, with one's own place on earth.

*   *   *

In Chapter 1, I tried to point out lingering vestiges of attention to intradependence that have characterized rural neighborhoods through the centuries. I also attempted to describe a common denominator in all types of rural decline: the individual orientation in liberal thinking. I have not said much about that thus far in dealing with conceptions of time. But the demise of cyclic time is deeply entwined with our cultural embrace of individualism, and we must recognize this if we are to remedy the problems connected to linear time.

I did mention, briefly, in this chapter, that a money economy lends itself to the mass participation of individuals as economic actors. Families, even neighborhoods, prior to the development of the money economy, were seen as primary in this regard. There's no hiding the fact that there is widespread concern about this. It has led to a "crisis of meaning" in the lives of many. In rural areas, this is particularly clear. There, we speak of saving the *family* farm as an economic entity. Even in cities we hear occasional references to *family* businesses, and again, there can be no denying the implied message: This is an institution that we ought to cling to lest it disappear forever.

But, alas, though everyone supports the family farm, though everyone is all for community, "we can't," we repeatedly tell ourselves, "stop progress"; or, to use another popular expression, "we can't stop the march of time." As it turns out, the demise of cyclic conceptions of time, like the demise of a sense of community, is tied to the individual orientation in liberal thought.

Let me refer, once again, to the development of liberalism chronicled in the introduction. Starting with a subtle inward turn heralded by St. Augustine in the fourth century and culminating with Herder's thoughts about the uniqueness of every individual in the eighteenth century, a communal orientation to life, to what makes it worth living, was slowly dismantled. Linear time had a hand in this. In order to get a feel for how this played out imagine that you once looked at time as something that reappeared everyday instead of something that marches on, never to be regained. It helps, I believe (although the analogy is not perfect), to try to think about time the way we currently do about the air that we breathe. It is possible, in theory, to measure the air that we breathe, and it is obvious that those who die young will breathe far less of it than those who die old, just as those who die young will spend far less time on earth. If the idea of measuring the air one will use on earth sounds absurd, then you are beginning to get a feel for how foreign the idea of measuring time must have been. After all, measuring time is a greater abstraction than measuring air. But the mechanical clock hid the abstract nature of the enterprise and made it concrete: Time had been used (at idleness or at work) once the hands on the clock had moved a certain distance.

In this way, time became linear. Although the clocks themselves were circular (though with digital technology this has changed), it gradually came to be accepted that time was not. The clock provided indispensable evidence that an hour of one's life had passed and that one could never relive that particular hour. If you combine this circumstance with Herder's idea that there is a unique *me*, that I must live *my* life *my* way, then you can see how easy it was for individuals to come to feel that time was their possession: I will spend *my* time on earth *my* way. It does not take much to see the anticommunal dimension in this development. When one of the key questions in life becomes "How are you going to spend your time?" or "How much is your time worth?" and we live in a society that believes that the individual pursuit of material accumulation is the highest sort of societal contribution and, further, when we even find sanction for this feverish accumulation in contemporary interpretations of Christian doctrine, then attention to one's community is bound to suffer.

And suffer it has. "Why should I spend my time working on a community project?" The result of embracing an individually oriented liberal worldview is that a culture of narcissism, as Christopher Lasch called it,[7] is created. That is, we have become a society of individuals obsessed with ourselves. Regrettably, our schools serve as one of the strongest engines promulgating this worldview. Instead of learning how to become a part of their community, instead of learning about how they might contribute to it, schoolchildren learn about their own individual strengths and weaknesses. In fact, we can't identify them early enough or fast enough. We run our kids through a battery of tests before they are eight years old, and then we call in the parents so that we can "interpret the scores." "Your child has some difficulty identifying concepts," one can often hear at these sessions. Ten years of anxiety and anguish are sure to follow this assessment. We practice a kind of hyperindividualism in our schools, and it is a testament to the resiliency of children that more lives are not ruined in the process.

If rural communities are to thrive, or even merely survive, they must put an end to the emphasis on individualism; they must put an end to their role as agent in the promotion of a culture of narcissism. I have much more to say about this in Part Three of this book. For now, I would like to make the point that rural schools can begin to create a path that others who are interested in doing something about the adverse psychological and cultural effects of our individually oriented worldview might follow. Answering to a conception of time derived from the cyclic rhythms in one's place is a potential first step toward returning a measure of health and vitality to rural schools, communities, and American society as a whole.

At the risk of oversimplifying a complex matter, I would like to close this chapter by suggesting a connection between something that is widely known, at least intuitively, and something that is not. Most people generally recognize that meaning or fulfillment in a human life is inevitably tied to the quality of the relationships a person creates with others. What is generally less recognized, however, is that there are but two phenomena that bring humans together in a way that relationships may be created. One is time and the other is place. Clearly, mobility related to our jobs, electronic media, the explosion of telecommunication options, and so forth have all severely diminished the role of place in our lives. Time, therefore, is now the phenomenon that brings people together. And time, when conceived as linear (which has been our cultural druthers, if you will), is fleeting. Our relationships, therefore, are temporary. In turn, the meaning that sustains our lives is diminished. Lives without commitment to much of anything, particularly when bolstered by economic, political, and educational theory premised on individualism, become increasingly egocentric, and the culture, therefore, becomes increasingly degenerate. One should logically expect prisons to become a predictable part of the landscape in such a society, and regrettably, such is our current state of affairs.

The solution to this predicament, I believe, is to reinsert place into the lives of most Americans. There are many ways that this might be done, and later in the book I will discuss several of them. For now, I'd like to point out that several years ago Wendell Berry predicted that if cultural healing was to take place in this country, it would need to begin in the countryside.[8] In this book, I intend to take this idea one step further and suggest that this healing will need to begin in the schools of the countryside.

3

The Avoidance of Risk

Destroy our farms and the grass will grow in the streets of every city in the country.

—*William Jennings Bryan, 1896*

Get big or get out.

—*Earl Butz, 1972*

Robert Fulgham, in his popular essay *All I Really Need to Know I Learned in Kindergarten*,[1] demonstrated how wonderful it is to be in a kindergarten classroom where every student can answer the teacher's question, every student can sing, and every student can play a theatrical role. Between that time and high-school graduation, the number who can do these things becomes incredibly small. Something happens along the way. It's not the case that an innate laziness overtakes these students; it's not the case that home life turns bad and parents lose the "parenting skills" that up until kindergarten had apparently been quite sufficient. It is something far more complex, far more subtle, and it, too, like the demise of cyclic time, is related to the ascendancy of the individual orientation in liberal thought. The widespread student indifference in the classroom, I believe, has more to do with the concept of risk than anything else.[2]

When the pursuit of individual interests is what is prized, then the message sent is that the risk is OK since it affects only the individual. By contrast, if individual contributions to the welfare of the community are what is prized, then whatever risks are involved take on far greater significance. Since the ramifications of this dynamic are far-reaching, I would like to take a little time to work it through before returning to the question of indifference in the classroom.

Cyclic conceptions of time, as we saw in the last chapter, hinged on their connection to nature. In the switch to linear time, the connection to nature was severed and humankind's outlook on life became increasingly "anthropocentric." That is, humans began to look at themselves as in some way dissociated from all other life on the planet. Before the ascendancy of this worldview in the seventeenth century, there was much greater attention paid to the role of nature in political, economic, and educational deliberation. After the seventeenth century, this attention diminished markedly. The requirement of finding a natural harmony, a kind of overall pattern between the affairs of humans and the physical world (as in, say, the ratio between the number of acres and the number of animals required to adequately manure the soil) was downplayed in favor of an outlook that objectified nature and thereby rendered it a mere source of wealth and production. The emphasis was not on overall pattern but on reductionism, the identification of parts. If tinkering with the parts of the natural world improved the short-term prospects of humankind, then it was in the interest of science to do the tinkering. Francis Bacon, for instance, argued that "the legitimate goal of science is the endowment of human life with new inventions and riches."[3]

The emphasis on individualism, the "right" to ever-greater riches and the inattention to nature that came with it, the idea of science as the key to labor-replacing technology, the powerful emphasis placed on freedom and autonomy—all of these things led to a kind of cultural stamp of approval for entrepreneurial fearlessness. As early as the eighteenth century, Jonathan Swift, through the publication of *Gulliver's Travels*, attacked this growing sentiment because in his view it resulted in a very unwise propensity to manipulate nature. His severe critique, however, went largely unnoticed; indeed, the work was frequently referred to as a children's book.

Heeding no warnings, individuals increasingly began to think of themselves as actors on the world unencumbered by communal obligations or traditions. By Swift's day, the wealthy began to move into neighborhoods of their own. Before this, rich and poor alike had lived in the same vicinity. In the late eighteenth-century movement toward residential segregation, it is possible to identify a trend among the emerging middle class to pursue the trappings of aristocratic life. In short, life became a kind of competition, not for subsistence or survival, but for the prize represented by wealth and all the circumstances it afforded.

Educational thought followed suit. By reading the papers of Massachusetts public-school founder Horace Mann, one can come to appreciate the extent to which it was believed that public schools were needed to turn potential paupers into successful competitors in the economic competition called the "marketplace." Because communal responsibilities were put on the back burner, there was room for risk taking of some consequence in the competition that slowly began to redefine life. The greater the risk, the greater the potential payoff. In a way that would have made no sense at all in a communally oriented world, entrepreneurs—those willing to take risks—gradually came to be viewed as the greatest contributors to the welfare of society. It took Adam Smith's eighteenth-century economic treatise, *The Wealth of Nations*, to turn this counterintuitive development into what came to be accepted as common sense. It is still conventional wisdom, for instance, to believe that in order to be successful, one needs to take risks. The slow movement of the term "successful" into perhaps the greatest accolade one may use to describe an individual has coincided with our increasingly pervasive tendency to view life as a kind of competition. It is important, I believe, to compare this term with the greatest sort of accolade one might have earned in an agrarian, communally oriented world. Before moving to that contrast, however, I'd like to return to the question of indifference in the classroom.

Schools take this ostensible truism about success and risk very seriously, for we have designed schools so that they structure in significant risk for students on a daily basis. What happens between kindergarten and highschool graduation is that we weed out those insufficiently prepared to take risks, which is to say, we weed out most children in the building. This is quite unintentional, of course. We teachers are rarely aware of the process. Convinced that we have the knowledge our children must come to know, we ask them in front of their peers if they can, in fact, provide us with the right answer. After years' worth of having the wrong answer, years' worth of being told they are incorrect, and years' worth of risking a shot at the right answer only to have another small chunk of their self-esteem erode away, students become silent, indifferent, unaffected by what is going on in the classroom. Those with greater stamina for taking risks survive the process. Although they may not be any more intelligent (as conventionally defined), they have learned to work the system we call schooling. They are headed for advanced placement, for programs for the gifted and talented, and ultimately, they will move on to the interesting jobs in society (which is to say, nearly synonymously, to jobs in urban and suburban America).

Steadfastly clinging to our one-answer view of knowledge, a view born of the reductionism inherent in the seventeenth-century scientific revolution, we slowly transform our students into unchallenged, disinterested, passive classroom drones. And then we berate them for their laziness or for the ostensible shortcomings of their parents.

Part of the industrial culture in which we and our schools are so deeply entwined has included the glorification of risk taking. And as I intend to show in this chapter, this puts rural students in a disadvantaged position, for one of the continuities of agrarian life, one that still lingers today in rural places, is the avoidance of risk.

* * *

I would like to return now to the development of the term "successful" as one of the nicest things we can say about someone. It wasn't always this way. Few individuals were referred to as successful in Thomas Jefferson's day. It simply wouldn't have occurred to his contemporaries, just as it no longer occurs to us to refer to someone as "virtuous." I have written hundreds of letters of recommendation for students, and I can say with absolute certainty that I have never referred to any of them as virtuous. Yet the term was widely used in Jefferson's day.

What's at work here? Actually, this is a nice example of the power of culture. As we have embraced liberal tenets more tightly than ever in this society, that is, as we have more steadfastly clung to an individual orientation to life, as we have defined life plans as synonymous with competition in the race for material accumulation, and as we have elevated the status of the risk takers among us, the accolade "successful" has come to be a much better cultural "fit" than the accolade "virtuous." Virtue speaks of attention to shouldering one's obligations to others and is therefore more at home in a community-oriented worldview. Success, by contrast, confines itself to the level of the individual.

It is worth carrying this analysis just a little further, for we can identify a few other traits of those among us who are most frequently labeled successful. In many cases, successful people follow a mobile career path. That is, they go where they see opportunity for ever-greater material gain. There is a risk-taking element to this. It is not easy to pack up and move to a new city, a new job, a new set of relationships. But this is part of the price successful people pay. "You only live once," we are ceaselessly told, and that phrase demonstrates our embrace of linear time while exposing the crisis of meaning that inevitably shadows an overly individualistic outlook on life.

Care and concern for the well-being of a place, particularly a shared place (the intradependence that is community, in other words) is conspicuously absent in our mobile society—and our society is governed by successful people. Using this seemingly harmless cultural shift in terms of what constitutes a popular accolade provides another window through which we can examine the disintegration of intradependence, cyclic conceptions of time, and the subject of this chapter, the avoidance of risk. To better understand this last topic, however, it is useful to reexamine the genesis of modern liberal economics.

* * *

As noted earlier, people who had an agrarian worldview took a dim view of high-risk innovation, and for good reason. For centuries, the avoidance of risk was an expression of allegiance to one's neighbors or one's community. This circumstance, I believe, was at the very root of the deep-seated conservatism among peasants, a phenomenon so obvious across Europe that historians have ceased to debate it.[4] The fascinating thing about U.S. rural history, particularly Midwest rural history, is that the roots of this conservatism were brought into the interior regions that made up the Old Northwest only to enter an ideological milieu that was openly critical of conservatism.

The most severe blow to the agrarian ethic of avoiding risk was the Enlightenment celebration of progress. There is a tendency to think about progress as an idea that evolved quite naturally from a series of technological innovations that ostensibly possessed self-evident benefit for all. As noted earlier, however, technological innovations were made during the Middle Ages, although, unlike today, they were not all immediately embraced and thought of as clear advances for humankind. Rather, the idea of progress came to be discussed as inevitable in order to legitimate the largest risk one might be asked to undertake: the complete overthrow of the way politics, economics, and education had been managed for centuries. In other words, people were asked to bear the risk involved with the overthrow of feudalism. This risk was minimized by the claim that no matter what happened, mankind would inevitably progress. It is worth noting that this claim was made at the time of both the bourgeois revolutions to end feudalism and the Marxist revolutions designed to put an end to liberal capitalism.

As the idea of progress picked up steam (this can be read literally) through ever-more-powerful and ever-more-complex technological innovation, the ethic of avoiding risk was increasingly viewed as anathema. A crucial fundamental shift in worldviews surrounded this development, and it is worth a short digression in order to make it as clear as possible.

Human beings possess two choices that serve as guides or guideposts for present action. We can either look to the past or look to the future, but in either case we go through a process of constructing what it is we see. It doesn't take a genius to figure out which of these our culture has come to define as appropriate and which is viewed as inappropriate. To be accused of "living in the past" is a derogatory remark today, usually uttered with the intention of devaluing someone's opinion or inflicting a modicum of shame. "Look to the future" has become a piece of sage advice that most of us receive many times in our lives, especially while we are young and impressionable. Interestingly, the resulting ahistoricism in this society has created some serious cultural flaws. When the past is defined as unimportant, it no longer burdens us. Yet the results of history remain. Removing the burden of history (however artificially) has created a distressingly shallow American character. "I didn't kill any Indians," one occasionally hears, or, "I've never owned any slaves." These comments, though true enough, ignore the fact that the results brought on by those who did do such things continue to stare us in the face. The cultural healing that needs to come about in this society will take place only when we garner the character necessary to shoulder the legacy our ancestors left us. Unfortunately, in a culture unaccustomed to looking to the past, problems associated with looking to the future accumulate and intensify.

Looking to the past suggests the avoidance of risk. Looking to the future requires a celebration of risk taking. This brings us back to Adam Smith and liberal economics. For Smith, risk taking was good, and the danger that had shadowed it for centuries—the welfare of one's neighbors or one's community—was taken care of by his famous "invisible hand." The economist Herman Daly contends that Smith's invisible hand never emerged, that what came in its stead was an "invisible foot" that kicked the common good to pieces.[5] But if the invisible hand did exist, it existed to contribute to the welfare of the *nation*, as the title of Smith's book implies. The community was lost in this kind of economic reckoning. Indeed, communities have been dealt out of every hand since *The Wealth of Nations* was published in 1776.

Smithian economic theory led to the most far-reaching social changes. Individuals were unencumbered by the welfare of the community. Their contribution to the common good was the sum total of their pursuits and subsequent accumulation. Political theory trailed along nicely behind this. Government was designed merely to ensure that all had an equal shot at material accumulation and to adjudicate any difficulties that might arise when individual efforts in the marketplace clashed. Community, once again, was not a part of the liberal political project. The same came to be true in the arena of educational theory. As pursuing one's own self-interest came to be construed as the best contribution one might make to society and as political mechanisms were put into place to facilitate this, education gradually came to be construed as the provision of the wherewithal required for individual economic pursuits. Community, increasingly, played no economic role; it had no political power outside of its own borders; and it ceased to play any role in the curriculum and instruction afforded its youth. As noted earlier, community was dealt out of every hand. There should be no wondering why communities in this country have fallen on hard times.

There are a couple of additional points that require consideration if we are to carefully examine the disintegration of a risk-avoidance ethic. The first is that we now have what we might logically expect in a society that celebrates risk: a minimal number of "safe" places. For half of this century the entire global population lived with the risk of total annihilation. And though this possibility seems less likely today than it did ten years ago, it has in no way disappeared altogether. Add to this the tremendous risks related to the safe production of food and the availability of clean air and water, and it becomes obvious that today's society must deal with anxieties that were not particularly troublesome for large portions of human history. Indeed, in the absence of strong communities, risks of every kind have multiplied tremendously. Adequate health care is slipping away from millions and millions of U.S. citizens, dramatically increasing the number of needless deaths. Violent crime rates have risen markedly, creating huge prison populations and a drain on resources that might have been used to restore destroyed communities. In far too many places in this country, one now takes a risk simply by walking the streets after dark.

Although the connection between a culture that celebrates risk taking and a society defined by high levels of risk ought to be obvious, there is one final point to be made that is perhaps less apparent, and that is this: A culture of risk taking deals a severe blow to democracy. An atmosphere marked by high levels of uncertainty is not good as far as the health of the human psyche is concerned. Yet a risk-taking culture creates uncertainty at an alarming rate. If history tells us anything, it is that humankind is at its worst when faced with uncertainty. One need only look at the circumstances that ushered in the political careers of individuals like Napoleon, Hitler, and Stalin to see this connection.

But one could look closer to home. The 1930s depression was a telling circumstance in this regard. A severe drought that lasted several years turned out to be a devastating blow to many farmers in the states of the trans-Mississippi West. Coupled with the worst financial depression in the nation's history, the catastrophic "dust bowl" drove many off the land. The West Coast was the primary destination of the five hundred thousand or so migrants who quit farming in states like the Dakotas, Nebraska, Kansas, Oklahoma, and Texas during this decade.

What came to be known as the "Okie" migration demonstrates what people are capable of doing under high levels of stress and uncertainty. Prior to this time period, Americans had subordinated and segregated ethnic minorities such as Mexican Americans and African Americans. Anglo Caucasians, however, had escaped this treatment and had enjoyed a comparably privileged status on the basis of their skin color. All of this changed in short order in California of the 1930s, and to a lesser degree, in Oregon and Washington. For the first time in our nation's history, large groups of white, Anglo-Saxon, Protestant Americans found themselves shunned by others of the same background. Signs appeared, like the one in the

Bakersfield Theater in California, saying such things as "Niggers and Okies Upstairs" or "No Okies Allowed." Blockades went up to prevent Okies from entering various communities. Special classes were created in schools to segregate the children of those who had made this migration.[6]

Although there was some variation in the kind of reception afforded Okies up and down the West Coast, no historian would dispute the claim that Okies were treated undemocratically. It is interesting to note that several "commissions" were created to study the "Okie problem." This is symptomatic of how democracy begins to erode in a high-risk atmosphere. The desire for certainty of outcomes is intensified when the risks are high. Under these conditions, people are willing to defer to "experts" or expert commissions in the hope that despite the risk, the desired outcome will be achieved. People will readily hand over enormous power with no strings attached if they deem the uncertainty they face to have reached an intolerable level.

* * *

It should be clear that a society that celebrates risk taking structures in some serious problems. It may be useful to work through an example of how this shakes out in a rural community.[7] A young couple just starting out buys out, on favorable terms, the operation of one of their parents. After several years of hard work, the couple decides to expand when a neighboring farmer retires. The couple soon discovers that the additional acres require larger machinery. After increasing their debt load to acquire the machinery, they discover that the machinery would pay for itself more quickly if there were additional acres to work. With several farmers in the vicinity in this expanding mode, the price of land and land rent rises dramatically. In the meantime, individuals of modest means are effectively denied access to the farming profession.

I should add here that for many decades now this process has been jump-started by our nation's farm policies. In part, expanding farmers are confronting the dictates of a policy designed to keep the price of food low while it maximizes the profits of key agribusiness firms. But they are also responding to what our culture prizes—individual entrepreneurs willing to take risks. It is interesting to note what happens during the process of farm expansion. First, intradependence erodes. With so many acres to attend to, farmers must work quickly, utilizing many petrochemical shortcuts. The result has been that it is becoming increasingly difficult to find farming areas that have not been seriously damaged from an ecological perspective. The health of the shared place is simply no longer a community concern. Second, the rhythmic, cyclical nature of farming work disappears. Time comes to dominate the expanded farm in much the same way as it does the factory. With large numbers of acres to plant, making the most of dry spring days becomes a race against the clock. If there is too much rain, the result could be financial disaster. This circumstance demonstrates the third effect, that enormous risks, both financial and ecological, are undertaken every year on expanded farms.

What this hypothetical, albeit typical, story of farm expansion represents is the disintegration of intradependence, cyclic time, and the avoidance of risk. I use a farming example in a book about rural schools in order to demonstrate that schools are profoundly affected by the circumstances that affect their communities. As the story of farm expansion has proceeded over the past half-century, fewer and fewer people have come to own larger and larger farms. The connection between this circumstance and depopulation within farming villages should be obvious. With fewer farm families in the countryside, fewer main-street businesses were required. And further, fewer children enrolled at the local school. But this does not exhaust the educational ramifications of farm expansion. The property tax burden, of which schooling expenses often represent the lion's share, has also fallen into fewer and fewer hands. Whereas once this burden was far more evenly distributed across the residents of a farm community, it now increasingly falls on fewer people. As one might expect, this can become a heavy burden, so one often finds that individuals running for school boards in rural communities do so with the express purpose of keeping school taxes down. It is not difficult to see that sometimes, at least, this intent can be at odds with the proper supervision of the intellectual life of local youth.

* * *

Now we're ready to return to Fulghum's question regarding why seniors in high school have lost the abilities they possessed in kindergarten. As I said earlier, I believe that we have structured in far too much risk in the public schools. There we have the strange phenomenon of teachers continuously asking questions and seeking answers that they already know. It's a very unnatural act that has no parallel or analogue in what teachers and students alike have come to call "real life." We do it merely to put an individual on the spot, to discover whether the individual "knows" a particular piece of information. There is no reason that this telling-then-asking pedagogy must dominate our instructional practices, other than that it lends itself well to the cultural transformation that has taken place in this country regarding what education is and what it is for.

It is preparation for life, we often hear—as if this takes the question out of the realm of what can be legitimately debated. And since life is a kind of individual competition for material accumulation (the winners receiving the accolade "successful"), we have made a competition out of schooling, and we have made it steadfastly an individual undertaking (to the point that getting help with homework is sometimes considered cheating). Questions with known answers legitimate our categorization of students into everything from gifted to disabled—the winners and losers in the competition called schooling. Generally speaking, no one wants to be a loser, but students risk this for twelve years. Every time the teacher calls on a student, the threat is there. Every time a test is given with directions to produce or identify the right answer, the threat is there.

In response, the mass of students move into an open space between winners and losers. They study enough or do enough homework to keep from becoming losers, but they don't accept the risk involved in coming to be seen as winners. Winners have to supply the right answer, which means they shoulder a certain amount of risk on a daily basis.

In this way we have produced schools that conveniently mirror the bell curve, with a few students at the top and a few at the bottom and with the issue of intelligence scarcely coming into the picture. Through the process we call schooling, risk takers garner the esteem necessary to be deemed successful. Interesting jobs and important decisions await them. Their understanding of their own community, let alone the role a community might play in a democracy, is nil, and the ramifications of this will be further community disintegration in the future.

* * *

It is important to see how intradependence, cyclic time, and the avoidance of risk have gradually been diminished in the face of modern liberal ideas about what life is, what it's about, what makes it worth living, and so on. An excessively individual orientation to life creates a culture of narcissism, to use Christopher Lasch's phrase once again. This kind of culture is ecologically and psychologically unhealthy, and we are only very gradually coming to understand the extent of our ill health.

I have tried to argue here in Part One that (1) intradependence, cyclic time, and the avoidance of risk—three agrarian communal characteristics—were once a vital part of the health and well-being of communities, (2) that these characteristics, though in severe decline, still linger in rural portions of the United States, and (3) that the decline of these characteristics has coincided with the rise of an industrial worldview predicated on liberal notions about what constitutes a self, about how to best orchestrate an economy, about what the proper role of government is, and increasingly, about education construed as training for successful competition in the economic market.

Without an adequate understanding of the third point just mentioned here, the first two points cannot form the basis for reconstituting rural schools with a particular focus on their community and their place on earth. Since that is the subject of this book, we will turn now to look at what I call "indispensable history," that is, rural history engaged from outside of a national, industrial, or urban perspective.

Part Two

Public Policy and the Subordination of Community

4

The Deserted Village: A European Prelude

We have profoundly forgotten everywhere that cash-payment is not the sole relation of human beings.

—*Thomas Carlyle, 1843*

It is important to see the connection between our cultural fascination with the future and our diminished perceptions regarding the worth of the past. Young adults majoring in history at colleges and universities across the country are routinely asked "What are you going to do with *that*?" The quip is familiar and demonstrates two pervasive, though lamentable, cultural assumptions. The first is that education should properly prepare one to step into a particular job, and the second is that the study of history is almost useless in any case. Paradoxically, even history majors preparing to become history teachers will frequently complain about a requirement to study educational history during the course of their teacher preparation program. The result in this instance is that prospective teachers move into their careers with no intellectual understanding of how the contours of their professional lives came to be shaped (a significant obstacle to be overcome if any of them should ever wish to change those contours). In the absence of this type of understanding, one easily falls into an assumption that holds that things "naturally" evolve into the way they are. In other words, the standard formula—six classes, a study hall, and a prep period—is pretty much the way things have to be. At a macro or societal level, this assumption plays itself out with huge disparities between the rich and the poor being routinely considered a circumstance that is just naturally so.

The point is that there is a price to be paid for our cultural inattention to the past. That price is a limitation on our freedom in this country. Although this is regrettable, we can't say that we weren't warned. Jefferson's admonition has been heard by almost all of us at one time or another: "If a nation expects to be both ignorant and free, it expects what never was and never will be."

The goal of Part Two of the book, titled "Public Policy and the Subordination of Community," is (1) to chronicle the rural history that preceded and followed the liberal philosophy discussed in Part One, (2) to demonstrate how this history has indeed created severe impediments to community vitality in this country, and finally, (3) to connect the ramifications of this history to a school-based attempt at recovering those lingering communal continuities that represent our best hope for restoring diminished and destroyed communities in this country.

We begin the story in Europe because it is impossible to reach an adequate understanding of early American history without an appreciation of its European antecedents. Since the early American experience was so totally tied to developments in England, we will focus most of our attention there.

* * *

I noted earlier that the twelfth and thirteenth centuries represent enviable periods in terms of sustainable yet productive agriculture. This development was in part tied to new technologies that were gradually embraced by northern European peasants after the year 1000. These changes included new strategies for rotating crops, new plows, and a new draft animal (the horse) and new harnesses designed for it.[1] By the end of the thirteenth century, sustainable agricultural productivity began to gradually diminish. Lords pushed hard to put more and more land into production in order to tap a growing urban market for food and fiber. This pressure marked the origin of what was later called "enclosure," or the process of fencing in (with stone or more often with a hedge) large or small portions of land that had historically been kept in "common." There was tremendous variation surrounding early enclosures (1400–1550) in particular. In one vicinity, the common land might be divided up into patches worked by particular neighborhood families. In another, the common land might not be suitable for crop agriculture and would therefore be used for pasturing the stock belonging to neighborhood families. An enclosure took place when someone acquired (through a variety of arrangements) all or part of the local commons, fenced it, and attempted to more intensely farm that particular piece of ground, more often than not by using it to raise sheep. Sometimes these acquisitions occurred with the consent of all of those who were affected by it; sometimes it did not. In later enclosures (1650–1800), there was often considerable opposition that was routinely overridden, with support from parliamentary legislation.

By the sixteenth century, England had begun to distinguish itself as a world contributor in the area of textiles production. The growth of this industry led to tremendous demand for sheep's wool. Thus, enclosures often took land out of tillage, reducing the need for agricultural laborers. The end result was depopulation in the countryside. Thomas More described this process in his famous *Utopia*, published in 1516. He argued that sheep

> which used to require so little food, have now apparently developed a raging appetite, and turned into man-eaters. Fields, houses, towns, everything goes down their throats. To put it more plainly, in those parts of the kingdom where the finest, and so the most expensive wool is produced, the nobles and gentlemen, not to mention several saintly abbots, have grown dissatisfied with the income that their predecessors got out of their estates. They're no longer content to lead lazy, comfortable lives, which do no good to society—they must actively do it harm, by enclosing all the land they can for pasture, and leaving none for cultivation. They're even tearing down houses and demolishing whole towns—except, of course, for the churches, which they preserve for use as sheepfolds.[2]

In the wake of More's *Utopia*, protesters often spoke of sheep as "people-eaters." One such individual, Thomas Bastard, wrote in 1598:

> Sheep have eaten our meadows and our downs,
> Our corn, our wood, whole villages and towns.[3]

It is all too clear that the enclosure movement served to promote business interests at the expense of the masses of people involved in agriculture. This pattern has yet to be broken in England or the United States.

There is much historical debate concerned with enclosure. Certainly, there are many apologists who claim that although it was a process not without costs, the benefits far outweighed them. We should acknowledge, too, that in the early years of the movement, the enclosure process allowed some peasants to acquire small holdings of their own. But it is stretching things to argue that enclosure in some way signaled the end of peasant lives for the masses of England's agricultural laborers.

There were other circumstances involved in that development. For instance, the fourteenth century was a period marked by many peasant rebellions across England and western Europe. Tired of what they took to be excessive tithes, taxes, and other restrictions on their livelihoods, thousands of peasants, led by the fiery John Ball, marched on the city of London in 1381. In response, some concessions were made by young King Richard II.

With what seemed like reasonable concessions in hand, the crowds gradually dispersed. To their dismay, the peasants went back to their homes and fields to find their lords enraged and poised to impose even greater hardships on them. Calling for a response from the king shortly thereafter, the protesters were told Richard's apparent reply, "Villeins [peasants] thou art and villeins thou shalt remain."[4]

As it turned out, none of the fourteenth-century peasant rebellions across Europe was successful in dramatically altering the status quo. But it is perceptible in retrospect that the accumulated effect of these many terrible rebellions against Europe's landed aristocracy forced concessions that eventually improved the quality of life for many peasant families.

There is another fourteenth-century circumstance to consider that is related to the gradual demise of feudal serfdom. The bubonic plague, or the Black Death, was an enormously catastrophic scourge that wiped out fully one-third of Europe's population. One result of this was that there was a great shortage of agricultural labor. Indeed, much of the land that had recently been put under the plow simply reverted to forest because there were no workers available to keep it in cultivation. This circumstance permitted two things to happen. The first was that a few peasants were able to acquire small holdings of their own, and the second was that in the face of such labor scarcity, peasants were able to make some successful demands on their lords.

The sum total of these developments was that the fourteenth and fifteenth centuries marked the beginning of the end of medieval serfdom.[5] There is clearly much to applaud in this development, but for our purposes, there is also much to be cautious about and to study and reflect upon. For example, William Cobbett, an early nineteenth-century observer, put the matter this way:

> Hume and other historians rail against the feudal system; and we, "enlightened" and "free" creatures as we are, look back with scorn, or, at least, with surprise and pity to the vassalage of our forefathers. But if the matter were well-inquired into, not slurred over, but well and truly examined, we should find that the people of these villages were as free in the days of William Rufus [a particularly brutal eleventh-century Norman-born English King] as are the people of the present day; and that vassalage, only under other names, exists now as completely as it existed then.[6]

This passage underscores two points that I would like to make as clear as possible. One is made implicitly by Cobbett, the other explicitly. Both are important themes for this book. First, with the passing of the feudal system—and this is seen most dramatically in the centuries-long enclosure movement—*care for the land was increasingly moved away from being a*

community or neighborhood responsibility to being an individual concern.
Second, Cobbett does not say this explicitly, but the issue of freedom that
he does raise is tied to the meaning that accompanies a life spent in com-
pliance with obligations that enhance the well-being of one's family, neighbors, and friends. The issue of freedom from David Hume's perspective is
freedom from coercion, or the freedom of not having anyone tell you what
you have to do. Certainly peasants didn't enjoy Hume's notion of freedom.
And yet Cobbett claims that they were as free as the ostensibly free agricultural laborers of England's nineteenth century. How can this be? This is
a complicated question, but we must sort through it if we are to take all the
guidance we can from the past in our attempt to renew rural schools.

Using a distinction made later by such accomplished political philosophers as Isaiah Berlin and C. B. Macpherson,[7] Cobbett is speaking of positive freedom, whereas Hume is referring to negative freedom. Negative freedom is the "freedom from" coercion, or being told what one can and
cannot do. Positive freedom is the "freedom to" maximize the personal development that accrues from shouldering responsibility in a web of social
relations. Negative freedom is individual based; positive freedom is community based. In other words, for Cobbett, freedom is not that which enables us to walk away from our home or job (negative freedom), but rather
is that which allows us to do those things that give joy and meaning to our
lives (positive freedom). The ethic of shared obligation for a particular
place—intradependence—is, at least for Cobbett, an expression of human
freedom. As the enclosure movement progressed, the peasantry was gradually abolished. On the surface, this looks to be an extension of freedom, but
only if freedom is defined as the absence of coercion. If freedom is defined
as the presence of joy and meaning in one's life, then the question is not so
easily settled.

The famous British historian R. H. Tawney made a point that seems to
mirror Cobbett's view of the matter: "Villeinage [peasantry] ceases but the
Poor Laws begin."[8] The collapse of the peasantry, which should have meant
the wide extension of freedom to the men and women of the English countryside, ironically meant widespread aimlessness and joblessness in growing
industrial centers. Poor Laws were created in an effort to curb the resulting
high levels of crime by keeping displaced rural dwellers occupied on poor
farms or in poorhouses.

In time, the circumstances of those adversely affected by enclosure would
less obviously reflect the fact that rather than an award of freedom having
taken place, something closely akin to its opposite was going on. But it is
my contention that this dynamic has become a defining characteristic of
rural history nevertheless. As large-scale industrial interests have intruded
in the countryside, those who dwell there have become less free, not more
so. This theme will become clearer in subsequent chapters.

*   *   *

Many of the individuals who will come to dominate the pages ahead are far from household names. Indeed, they represent little more than footnotes, if that, in the history texts our children read in school. This fact, in and of itself, merits serious inquiry. I'm told that H. G. Wells once said that whoever controls the present controls the past; whoever controls the past controls the future. If our history is written as the story of continual progress unmarred by our treatment of, say, the original inhabitants of this continent or the millions of African Americans we held in bondage, then our ability to gauge what constitutes social justice is markedly diminished. Although I do not wish in any way to put the injustices afforded white small farmers across Europe and the United States over several centuries on a par with the injustices inflicted upon various ethnic minorities, it is necessary nevertheless to explore the "unsettling" of the countryside (as Wendell Berry put it) in order to enhance our ability to understand rural circumstances and the sort of social justice that has created them.

The celebration of urban industrial progress in the pages of our history books contributes indirectly to the stereotype of rural places, and therefore rural people, as unimportant. Indeed, rural dwellers have been told time and time again that the disintegration of their communities, the boarded-up main-street businesses, the closed schools, and the growing sense of isolation are all a part of the price of progress. They are all somehow or other unavoidable or natural, and therefore those who make the decisions (and profit from them) that create these circumstances are blameless. It is necessary, I believe, to keep these issues in mind as we work through some rural history that most historians, apparently, have considered unimportant.

We begin with the career of Gerrard Winstanley in the first half of seventeenth-century England. It was a tumultuous time. Well over a century's worth of small and large enclosures had swelled the ranks of people England called "masterless men." At the same time, a growing commercialist class of merchants, bankers, lawyers, insurance dealers, and so on was beginning to dominate the political affairs of England's larger cities. Overwhelmingly made up of members of a dissenting religious tradition (Calvinism), this group found itself opposed to the Anglican landed interests in Parliament on many religious, economic, and educational issues. By 1642, King Charles I and his following among the nobility came to blows with the Presbyterian merchant classes that had gained control in the House of Commons. The English Civil War was the result. Many claim that this episode spelled the end of the feudal order in England.

Winstanley was born in Lancashire in 1605. His father was a cloth merchant. Although he finished grammar school, young Gerrard was unable to attend a university. At the age of twenty-five, he was apprenticed to a tailor named Sarah Gaters. Seven years later, he was admitted to the Merchant

Taylors Company as a free citizen of London. Little is known about Winstanley's early career in London except that his business suffered from the economic turmoil resulting from the civil war. In 1643 he took his family to Surrey, where he stayed with friends and earned his keep as a cattle herder. His writing career spanned only four years, but during that time he distinguished himself as a leading social critic. In 1652 he published *The Law of Freedom*, which, like *Leviathan*, the more famous treatise published by Thomas Hobbes in the same year, was a blueprint for Oliver Cromwell's consideration as lord protector of the new English republic.[9] Winstanley is best known, however, for his role as England's leading "digger," or "true leveler." He earned this distinction during spring and summer 1649.

Five harvest failures between 1645 and 1650, combined with the exigencies of civil war, rendered conditions in the English countryside most tenuous. Whereas many merchants profited from scarce goods, farmers, in general, suffered throughout the decade. These conditions took their toll on England's country people and contributed to the atmosphere of instability and uncertainty across the land. Many poor people began to rebel. One contemporary observer noted that "the poor did gather together in troops of 10, 20, 30 in the Roades, and seized upon Corne as it was carrying to market, and divided it among themselves before the owners faces telling them that they could not starve."[10] Winstanley and several of his followers took a more moderate course. A small group of masterless men (former peasants) met at St. George's Hill in Surrey on an unenclosed commons. It was poor land, little used by the neighborhood, and consequently Winstanley and company began digging the sod and planting beans, parsnips, and other staple crops.

Local landlords were incensed by the implications of what the diggers were doing. They called upon the newly formed Council of State to chase them away. Thomas Fairfax, one of Cromwell's prominent generals in the war against the king, spoke with Winstanley but was unable to convince him to give up the venture. Local landlords, however, soon took matters into their own hands. They staged night raids, burning huts that served as temporary housing and severely beating the diggers, who, pledged to nonviolence, did not resist. And they continually harassed the diggers with legal action. Winstanley, for example, was arrested and charged with trespassing on several occasions. Several diggers spent time in jail on trumped-up charges because they refused to employ a lawyer in their defense. With their numbers reduced, the diggers suffered through more night raids, resulting in more houses burned and crops destroyed, until at last they removed to Cobham Heath a few miles away. There, the legal and physical harassment continued until the experiment was abandoned in April 1650.[11]

Although there is some evidence that similar digger experiments got started in other locales across England, none was successful. Winstanley was devastated by the failure of the movement. He dropped out of the public eye until he published *The Law of Freedom* in 1652, his last attempt to change England for the better. Winstanley had been a free citizen of London, a cloth merchant familiar with the Puritan theology of his peers. When he was forced to move to the country in 1643, he was introduced to another world. It was a world of poor country people, and over the course of the 1640s, Winstanley came to the conclusion that these people were not depraved "vulgar masses," as they were so often called by the emerging urban merchant class. Nevertheless, the merchant class had internalized these views, according to Winstanley, as a result of the actions of others interested in the perpetuation of power.

To expose the psychological elements of oppression, Winstanley wrote about the "Norman yoke" as the scourge of British history. He wrote about the flaws in a theology that legitimized the election of a few through the damnation of many (Puritanism). Winstanley believed that if he could entice the poor of England to throw off the legacy of Normanism (which he often referred to as "Kingly power") and the idea that their material poverty was an indication of their religious depravity, the poor might then articulate a political agenda of their own. The concept of digger communities was designed with this end in mind.

Clearly the period between 1640 and 1660 in England was a historical moment ripe with possibility. The feudal order had crumbled, as demonstrated by the execution of Charles I. The ascendancy of mercantile power in the state, as outlined by Thomas Hobbes, opened up the world to a new economic order, yet it perpetuated, in Winstanley's view, the exercise of "Kingly power."

> While this Kingly power reigned in one man called Charles, all sorts of people complained of oppression, both Gentry and Common people, because their lands, enclosures, and copyholds were entangled, and because their trades were destroyed by monopolizing patentees . . . thereupon you called upon the poor people to help you, and cast out oppression; and that top-bough is lopped off the tree of tyranny, and Kingly power in that one particular is cast out; but alas oppression is a great tree still, and keeps off the sun of freedom from the poor commons still.[12]

Winstanley was not alone in this assessment. John Lilburne, disappointed by the failure of Cromwell to attend to the agenda of the commoners, published a scathing attack called *New Chains Discovered.* "Several former soldiers" of the parliamentary forces wrote and published *The Hunting of the Foxes,* wherein they maintained that monarchy "had lost its name but not its nature, its form but not its power, they making themselves as absolute as ever the King in his reign, dignity, and supremacy."[13] Although Winstanley and others tried to provide a blueprint for a community-oriented vision of liberalism, the ascendant vision was one wherein the nation rested not on strong communities but on an ever-increasing centralized power.

Winstanley's contribution to rural history is that he made it abundantly clear that there was an alternative to this ascendant liberal vision, though it was soundly rejected by those who came to power after the civil war. Winstanley's vision for an agrarian, democratic, community-oriented society was based on positive freedom and popular sovereignty. In turn, this society was premised on the inherent rationality of the individual, cultivated through education. This idea, resting the fate of a nation on human rational power refined through formal education, was one that Winstanley shared with many later Enlightenment spokespersons. Positive versus negative freedom, however, as well as the differences between state and popular sovereignty (the locus of decisionmaking power) and the extent to which land ought to be available to anyone, were issues that set Winstanley apart from many later influential philosophers.

When trying to weave together a cohesiveness or consistency between political, economic, and educational theory, Winstanley insisted, unlike Hobbes, Locke, and many others, that common preservation (vibrant community life) rather than self-preservation ought to be the first and most prominent measure of fit. For Winstanley, human nature was essentially social and ecological rather than individualistic and anthropocentric (the view that the earth is essentially at the disposal of humans). True freedom was not the pursuit of self-interest free from coercive interference, but as Winstanley put it, "true freedom lies in the free enjoyment of the earth."[14] The possession of land by a few impedes the commoners' capacity for self-determination. It is self-determination that constitutes freedom for Winstanley, a positive rather than negative conception, and self-determination is in turn contingent upon landownership, common preservation, and popular sovereignty.

Winstanley saw that at the very moment the modern version of liberalism was being created, the seeds of community disintegration were being planted. Without the benefit of the hindsight we can employ today, Winstanley knew that creating political, economic, and educational theory that hinged on self-preservation or maximizing self-interest would be destructive for people and their places.

There is another point to be made here. One frequently hears a lament these days about the collapse of morality or the loss of morals among youth in American society. We typically assign responsibility for this development to parents or possibly to schools, without recognizing that morality—the essence or quality of the relationships between people—is developed by apprehending and then protecting what is held in common. As the educational philosopher Dale Snauwaert has demonstrated, morality is premised upon "knowing the public interest and acting to preserve community life." That is, "moral development is by definition intimately connected to community."[15]

When a society openly embraces political, economic, and educational theory that hinges on an individualistic and anthropocentric conception of human nature, community disintegration is logical and predictable. What necessarily follows as well, however, is the eventual collapse of substantial moral development. This is a key point. Bolstered by our cultural fascination with the future, advocates of community restoration are frequently accused of being "nostalgic" or of "living in the past," and there can be no denying the pejorative connotation that accompanies these claims. But such charges are inordinately shallow, for those who make them fail to recognize the flimsy nature of the cultural assumptions that undergird their thinking. The restoration of rural (and other) communities is not a matter of nostalgia but is, rather, a practical necessity, particularly in a world such as ours, in which the resource base continues to empty at a rapid rate. Under the circumstances to come, the stakes premised on a moral citizenry are considerably heightened.

There is another way to make this point, and here I wish to borrow from Daniel Kemmis' analysis of comments made by the German philosopher Hegel.[16] Hegel was convinced that the history of the United States had nothing to offer civilization until the nation came to terms with the concept of limits. As long as people could push or be pushed further west, he argued, the nation would never have to face itself and work out an acceptable standard for the quality of human relationships. In other words, morality could be and was cast aside. It doesn't take much to demonstrate this. Crime, drug use, prison population, violence, rape, physical and sexual abuse of children, and so on—these are all rising at such incredible rates that they are increasingly seen from the outside as defining characteristics of our society.

Winstanley and his followers worked to put Europe's postfeudal society on a trajectory that would have led to a more desirable definition of who we are as a people. But as I have already noted, his ideas were soundly rejected by those who came to power after Charles I. His brilliant social analyses were largely forgotten during his own lifetime. His work was only "rediscovered," so to speak, during the twentieth century. Through the study of his thought and actions, however, we can acquire the insight necessary to view the way the countryside has been treated as something other than the march of inevitable progress.

*   *   *

Shortly after the English Civil War, a young physician named John Locke began delving into the arena of political and economic philosophy. His

Second Treatise on Government, officially published in 1690 but circulated in other forms much earlier, became an immensely influential argument for political and economic policy governed by the notion of the primacy of individual self-interest.

Locke brilliantly legitimated the unlimited accumulation of property in a society that was otherwise based on human equality. He charted a course for driving a wedge between Europe's interlocked churches and states, and he argued, logically, for the right to rebel and unseat any government that did not act in the interest of the people. In many ways, Locke provided the intellectual rationale for the architects of the colonial revolt against England and the eventual establishment of the United States. For this reason he is sometimes referred to as "America's philosopher."

It is necessary to take a hard look at how he managed to pull off these tremendous intellectual accomplishments if we are to understand the urban industrial worldview that he helped to refine and energize. Locke begins the *Second Treatise* by undercutting any power in the argument for the "divine right of kings." He points out quite persuasively that we have no way of telling whether royal families descended directly from Adam and Eve, the only argument that could possibly legitimate the divine right claim. We can think about what circumstances must have been like for humankind before there were states and governments, however. And through this process, according to Locke, we can identify what was available to early man and argue that whatever list we generate constitutes what is by nature a human *right.* Indeed, the "state of nature" was a popular point of philosophical discussion for Enlightenment-era thinkers. Talk of the "rights of man," to use Thomas Paine's phrase, led to the philosophical substitution of "natural" for "divine" law. By nature, all individuals had certain inalienable rights.

It doesn't take a great deal of analysis to discover that the theoretical assumptions undergirding the establishment of the United States were wrapped up in this kind of rhetoric. But it is important, too, to recognize the extent to which the talk of rights underscored an already pervasive individual orientation to life and living. Humans in the state of nature took what nature provided in order to survive. This ostensibly established the claim that humans are presocial and that self-preservation ought to be the standard that drives political, economic, and educational thinking. For example, natural man moves about enjoying the earth in common with others, but at some point he mixes his labor with the earth. Perhaps he picks some apples to eat. Through this process of mixing labor with the earth, a property claim is made; that is, the apples become his. "Labor put a distinction between them [the apples] and common. That added something to them more than Nature, the common Mother of all, had done; and so they became his private *right.*"[17]

For Locke, two natural laws constrain this process of private property creation and accumulation. One is that natural man was compelled to leave "enough and as good" for others in the vicinity. The other was that he could not take more apples than he could eat and thus had to leave some to spoil. If this had marked the end of his analysis related to property, however, rural history might have turned out far differently. To this point, nothing has been argued that might have provoked disagreement from the likes of an agrarian thinker like Winstanley. Indeed, with such constraints, England's enclosure movement would have been in serious jeopardy, for clearly the enclosure process left many without any land at all.

But Locke didn't stop there. He went on to argue that the creation of a money economy (something he saw as a natural development) nullified these two natural constraints. One could accumulate many more apples than one could possibly eat, since the ability to sell the excess apples for currency (which would not spoil) made this possible. The "enough and as good" principle fell before the money economy as well, or so it is possible to argue.[18] The freedom to accumulate in great excess of what would otherwise spoil legitimated vast improvements in agricultural production, most notably enclosures, for the man who works ten acres and produces as much food on it as would have been available on one hundred acres of unimproved land, can, according to Locke, "truly be said to give ninety acres to Mankind."[19]

The money economy makes all the difference. If land is unavailable for agricultural laborers, wages can be earned and exchanged for the food a person requires. Whether or not Locke articulated this theory of property with the intent of legitimating dispossession, it cannot be denied that it was a great boon to the architects of enclosures and that it set the modern world on a trajectory that came to consider the countryside as the appropriate locale for shouldering the burdens that accrued as the price of urban industrial progress.

One should not underemphasize the huge contributions Locke made to establishing free societies in the West. Although feudalism was crumbling prior to his arrival on the scene, Locke's pen provided the death blow. The stranglehold held by the interlocked interests of church and aristocratic state was broken. Using the power of Locke's arguments, the emerging industrial interests won their seats in the halls of power. But these accomplishments should not blind us to the serious problems that have shadowed the implementation of Lockean philosophy.

Because he used self-preservation rather than community preservation as a starting point, the individual quite naturally became the focus of his subsequent philosophy. If there was to be any meaning at all to the claim of universal human freedom for Locke, individuals would require certain rights. This idea would have been completely foreign to the Greeks and largely foreign to a community-oriented thinker like Winstanley. For the Greeks and for Winstanley, human fulfillment is tied to playing a satisfying role in a web of social relations. The emphasis is not on what rights one naturally accrues but on how one shoulders responsibility for the welfare of one's closest associations.

Here we can get a glimpse of the poverty of Locke's otherwise powerful philosophy. Beginning with an individual orientation limits the question of fulfillment to individual acquisition. That is, the path to a fulfilled life is simply marked by ever-greater levels of consumption. If the acquisition of ever more property is the name of the game, then what we do in the arena of politics and education must be structured to facilitate this goal. Government, ideally, will keep from interfering in man's pursuit of property and will adjudicate disputes when paths of pursuit cross. Education, in its turn, will provide the intellectual wherewithal for the successful pursuit of property while it serves as a playing field leveler.

Like Thomas Hobbes before him, Locke's individual orientation forces him into a negative conception of freedom as the absence of coercion or interference. For Locke, freedom is merely freedom *from*. For Winstanley, by contrast, freedom is conceived as freedom *to*. Although at first glance the difference may seem to be little more than a matter of semantics, the policy implications are enormous. One is conducive to policy that facilitates unfettered capitalist accumulation irrespective of how it might affect any particular community; the other is conducive to policy that maintains the primacy of community as the locus of human fulfillment. One connects freedom to the capability and competence developed throughout a working life, whereas the other connects freedom to the availability of wage labor or public assistance.

Perhaps a contemporary example will make the distinction between positive and negative freedom clearer and at the same time demonstrate that there is much more at stake than semantics. Jean Bethke Elshtain relayed the story of a Boston mother living in a low-income housing project saturated with violent crime. The mother worried about the safety of her three children, and for months she called the police as shootings occurred or when drug deals went down. After joining forces with other mothers, she convinced the police department to orchestrate a "stop and search" policy on periodic community "sweeps." But as the mothers rejoiced, the lawyers descended. Individuals in this society are guaranteed *freedom from* this kind of intrusion. The policy was over almost before it started. The mother of three propped mattresses in front of her windows in the vain hope that they would block the path of stray bullets that might otherwise take the life of one of her children. The *Boston Globe* discussed the issue of freedom from the point of view of the mother of three. She and her children were denied the right *to* sit on a stoop or at a playground. The right *to* walk to a store at any reasonable time . . . without the fear of getting caught in a cross fire. The right *to* spend a peaceful evening inside their own apartment. The right *to* stare out a window. The right *to* free association. The right *to* use a swing set whenever the whim strikes. The right *to* complain publicly against gangsters in their midst. The right *to* be rid of crack and cocaine in the hallway and vestibule. The right *to* life [emphasis added].[20]

* * *

It doesn't require much thought to see how the Lockean emphasis on possessive individualism could mesh well with the thought of seventeenth-century scientists like Bacon and Descartes, who argued that nature should become the slave of humans. And it requires very little additional analysis to see that the linking of these schools of thought was not a healthy prescription for the environment. Earlier Greek and Thomistic views about natural harmony and the human role in producing it were forthrightly dismissed. Henceforth, the earth was there for any person with the wherewithal to use it profitably, and this, Bacon and Descartes argued, was how it should be. Recall that this logic was employed throughout the eighteenth and nineteenth centuries in the United States to dispossess the original inhabitants of the continent. But that puts us ahead of the story.

Spurred on by the power of Locke's arguments, ever-larger enclosures were built throughout the eighteenth century, and these were facilitated by parliamentary legislation that made it increasingly easy to override the objections of those whom it would adversely affect. Former peasants drifted to burgeoning industrial cities in search of work. They were free, but free to do what? As the popular song claimed during the 1960s, "freedom is just another word for nothing left to lose."[21] Tawney forcefully reminded us that although the constraints traditionally imposed on peasant lives ceased to be, Poor Laws took their place. It is one of the great ironies of history that for the better part of two centuries, anyone who expressed reservation about the diminishment of the peasantry was accused of idolizing a harsh, demanding existence, as if the squalid lives led by former peasants in the ramshackle overcrowded housing of the growing industrial centers were not harsh and demanding. The evidence in this regard is both plentiful and telling, yet it is ignored by the defenders of progress, who for some reason rush to demean the "overly sentimental." A few passages from nineteenth-century observers of the housing available to former peasants in England's growing industrial centers will suffice: "Wretched hovels, little better than pigsties," remarked Cobbett. Friedrich Engels described the English industrial housing as "tottering filth and ruin that pass[es] all description." Robert Owen agreed that conditions were "terrible almost beyond belief . . . extremes of inhumanity utterly disgraceful, indeed, to a civilized nation." An English Poor Law Commission report stated, "The annual loss of life from filth and bad ventilation [is] greater than the loss from death or wounds in the wars in which the country has been engaged in modern times."[22] But as terrible as all of this sounds, there is an even more sorrowful dimension to the story. Central to the peasant's life was the acquisition of skill and competence in the great variety of a peasant's daily tasks. Removing peasants from the land meant that these attributes were of little use, and the low-paid work that awaited the vast majority of them was routine, monotonous, and required very little skill. An element of dignity was thereby removed from their lives. As one early twentieth-century student of village life remarked, "enclosure . . . left the people helpless against influences which have sapped away their interests, robbed them of security and peace, rendered their knowledge and skill of small value, and seriously affected their personal pride and their character."

Contemporaries were not blind to these developments. They saw, firsthand, the plight of England's rural poor. They lamented the demise of hundreds of small agricultural villages. One man, Arthur Young, made a career during the eighteenth century as an advocate of enclosure and large-scale agricultural production. Shortly before his death, however, he came to regret the results of his life's work: "I had rather that all the commons of England were sunk in the sea, than that the poor should in the future be treated on enclosing as they have been hitherto."[23]

Young's words nicely capture the fact that the history of the countryside has not been an onward and upward story. The mutuality that defined the quality of neighborhoodship, the celebrations that evolved out of what was otherwise demanding physical toil, the pride of accomplishment for work done well, for a community obligation well met—all of these dimensions of intradependence were stripped from peasants' lives. And time, too, was suddenly transformed into something vastly different than they had ever known. Instead of being at their disposal, time began to govern them. They were far from being their own masters: The clock told them when they would eat, sleep, and work. And last, of course, individuals well steeped in the wisdom of avoiding risk were forced to take the very largest risk of all; that is, they were forced to risk their lives in the filthy and disease-ridden industrial centers of England, all for the opportunity to work for small wages, to have twelve- to fourteen-hour workdays, six days a week.

It is imperative that rural dwellers understand the historical connection between the industrial system we have embraced in most Western countries, and the ill-treatment of the countryside that has come in its wake. If today's rural children are not permitted to sort through this history and tie it to their own circumstances, their sense of political efficacy and their allegiance to their homes, their places, and their neighbors and friends will never be what it might.

There is another irony in the fact that at one point in this country, this history was within the grasp of literally thousands of rural children. During the nineteenth and early twentieth centuries, when schooling was dominated by a recitation pedagogy, rural schoolchildren frequently recited the lines of an Oliver Goldsmith poem without sorting through its relevance for their own lives and circumstances. The poem is "The Deserted Village," and it is widely considered to be one of the most moving poems in the English language. The passage most often repeated is this one:

Ill fares the land, to hastening ills a prey,
Where wealth accumulates and men decay.[24]

Of course Goldsmith is considered a romantic, an individual who idolized a past that never was: The agricultural villages that dropped off the maps during England's eighteenth century were places where life cut close to the bone, where there was no joy, where there was only hardship and ceaseless toil; they were places that should have disappeared from the maps, or so the argument goes.

When all the circumstances are considered well, however, as Cobbett suggested, this last interpretation must be considered very convenient for those who derived the benefit from the demise of these places. This would not necessarily render it inaccurate, though I believe it is. It is an interpretation that seems to come all too easily from those wrapped up in Locke's all-powerful money economy, where pleasure is seen as a function of the profit one makes rather than as a function of the work one does. In Winstanley's economics, there was profit in work's pleasure. Although that may be a culturally foreign notion to us today, that doesn't change the fact that it could be a fundamental truth regarding the human condition and therefore a significant part of the antidote to our current cultural failings.

＊　　　＊　　　＊

The story of John Locke brings us up to the American scene, the subject of the next two chapters. But before moving on, it may be useful to draw one final connection between the history described in this chapter and the concept of intradependence discussed in Chapter 1. Within the notion of intradependence is the idea that what one does (that is, one's "work") fulfills a need that exists among those with whom the physical place is shared. This is part of what it means to be a member of a community. What communities do for individuals in return is to prescribe a social identity.[25] Those who have been raised in rural America may readily identify with this, as this is one of the few locales where intradependence lingers. Those raised in suburban areas will have more difficulty with this idea, since suburbs are virtually devoid of intradependence.

The social identity one comes to possess in an unhealthy community may well be hierarchical and based on class, religion, gender, ethnicity, wealth, occupation, and so forth. This is why, as I have argued in another work, a sense of place has not been far distant from a less ennobling characteristic—that is, a sense of knowing one's place. And it is also why, as Wes Jackson has reminded us, the restoration of communities that must take place in this country needs to be guided by different sets of assumptions than those that led to their initial settlement. This is an extremely important point, and it will be raised again further on. It is one of the reasons that education has (or ought to have) such a pivotal role in efforts at rural renewal.

But let's put aside just for a moment the potential for problems related to the configuration of communities of the past. And let's push the idea of communities providing a social identity just a little further. In a community that is truly a community, social identity is tied to one's contribution to the shared place, that is, one's work. Embracing Adam Smith and a national economy (and our subsequent embrace of an international economy) has removed the social identity that came with the contribution one made to the health and well-being of the community. In other words, when one's work contributes in some vague way to a national or international economy and not in any direct way to what is needed by one's friends and neighbors, the issue of social identity becomes extremely problematic. One's work becomes narrowly instrumental; that is, it becomes merely a means to acquire money ultimately for nothing other than leisure and pleasure. Although this may be good for a national or an international economy, it is poison for a community. Obligations disappear, allegiance erodes, we become "unencumbered selves," and, predictably, procedures kick in to take care of the tremendously disruptive fallout that stems from these developments.

5

The American Countryside and the Dynamics of Acquisition

A community is like a ship; everyone ought to be prepared to take the helm.
—Henrik Ibsen, 1882

We often forget that several American colonies were well established by 1649, the point at which Charles I lost his head and Winstanley and his fellow diggers planted their crops on St. George's Hill. Despite the fact that we like to think of our history as having been categorically different from that of Europe, in point of fact the English immigrants to America reproduced European feudal-like conditions in short order. Colonies designated official state churches, communities created restrictions stipulating that only those who had come from certain counties in England were allowed, and individuals like John Pynchon (discussed in Chapter 1) eventually acquired huge holdings. Slavery existed in all colonies, and this, combined with the prevalence of individuals serving seven or more years as indentured servants, meant that master-serf feudal relations became well entrenched.

As the eighteenth century progressed, however, the popularity of Lockean liberal ideas grew. Second- and third-generation colonials grew tired of the exploitive nature of England's relationship with its colonies. Each additional tax levied by Parliament throughout the middle decades of the eighteenth century brought more vehement discontent. After waging war on behalf of England with France and its Indian allies during the 1760s, the colonists found continued taxation without representation even harder to bear. The result, of course, was the Declaration of Independence and subsequent war with England. This story is familiar enough. But it is important to keep in mind that the American Revolution was Locke-inspired. In other words, the right of the individual to pursue and acquire unlimited amounts of property was a kind of guiding principle that was used to legitimate American separation from England, just as it was used to focus the building of American economic and political institutions. The merchant forces that defeated King Charles and then crushed Winstanley's liberal vision in England had their eighteenth-century counterparts in such commercially oriented people as Samuel Adams, Benjamin Rush, John Adams, John Hancock, and Alexander Hamilton. In many ways, the American Revolution was an expression of their power.

But things didn't go entirely their way. The settling of the American colonies came about as a result of some unique circumstances. To be sure, the Lockean notion of putting the land to good use and improve it in an effort to make a religious and humanitarian statement was an idea that led to some decidedly undemocratic behavior with respect to the native and African populations in America. But if we look beyond these dynamics, it is true that some democratic ideas were beginning to take root. In fact, in some obscure places we can begin to piece together a variant of Winstanley's vision for an agrarian (rather than an industrial) society, marked by an allegiance to popular sovereignty and an emphasis on positive freedom.

In his 1768 publication, *Letters from a Pennsylvania Farmer*, John Dickinson, a Philadelphia lawyer, wrote glowingly of the virtues of the small farmer and argued that frugality, thrift, and a propensity for the simple life would be the colonies' best weapon against an increasingly oppressive mother country. Likewise, New Yorker Hector St. John Crevecoeur established himself as a leading American agrarianist in his 1780 publication, *Letters from an American Farmer*. He, too, glorified the farming life and ascribed to it a special sort of virtue.

Virginians Thomas Jefferson and John Taylor were popularizers of a kind of agrarianism strong enough to check the power of the commercialist interests in the seaboard cities. Jefferson, in particular, marked himself as an heir to Winstanley in promoting an agrarian vision: "Those who labour in the earth are the chosen people of God, if he ever had a chosen people, whose breasts he made the peculiar deposit for substantial and genuine virtue." Seeking to avoid the problems associated with urban industrialism, he argued that American workshops should "remain in Europe ... the mobs of great cities add just so much support of pure government, as sores do to the strength of the human body."[1]

The voice of Thomas Paine also represents an exception to the domination of commercialist views. Echoing Jean-Jacques Rousseau and other Enlightenment thinkers in his speculation on "natural man," Paine wrote that "the most affluent and the most miserable of the human race are to be found in the countries that are called civilized." Going on to explain that "man did not make the earth," Paine reasoned that "though he had a natural right to *occupy* it, he had no right to *locate as his property* in perpetuity any part of it [Paine's emphasis]." Every human born, according to Paine, was endowed with a natural right to earth, air, and water. Paine felt that a national fund ought to be created that would give nonlandowners "the sum of fifteen pounds sterling, as a compensation in part, for the loss of his or her natural inheritance" upon reaching the age of twenty-one. In addition, they were to receive "the sum of ten pounds per annum, during life" until age fifty.[2] The rationale behind Paine's proposal is reminiscent of the philosophy of Gerrard Winstanley. Paine's ideas, like Winstanley's, were completely ignored.

For all of their talk of agrarianism in the middle colonies and in the South, it was in New England, the commercial hotbed of the new American confederacy, that we can get the clearest picture of the fate of agrarian thinking in this country and, consequently, the fate of the countryside as well. Daniel Shays' Rebellion, an eighteenth-century incident that receives little more than a casual mention in the history books our students engage in school, represents the American version of the plight of Winstanley and the English diggers. It is worth describing this debacle in some detail.

*   *   *

Daniel Shays was a self-effacing farmer. His name has gone down in U.S. history as the catalyst behind an ill-fated, haphazard rebellion in western Massachusetts. Historian David P. Szatmary provides an interesting chronicle of how the activities of Shays and his followers were interpreted by historians in the years following the rebellion. During the nineteenth century, historians typically chastised the rebels as vicious, ignorant fools. Later, during the depression of the 1930s, some historians took a more sympathetic view of the Shaysites, seeing the rebellion as a classic case of agrarian versus commercial interests. Still later, historians seemed to downplay this clash, arguing that the rebels were not rebels after all, that they were merely discontented folks who worked within the system for the most part, with the possible exception of a minor incident or two.[3]

If nothing else, Szatmary's book is important for illuminating the important issue of historical interpretation. What are we to make of Shays' Rebellion? How widely will we disseminate all the facts that are known about this debacle? By omitting or downplaying the size and scope of Shays' Rebellion, historians have rendered a verdict regarding what we are to make of it: We are to make nothing of it because it was not important, not worthy of serious study. For verification, one need only look at the treatment Shays receives in the history textbooks in American schools. In point of fact, Shays and his rebellion do not fit the onward and upward story we have made of public-school history. In this history, Daniel Shays may be an interesting footnote, perhaps, but he doesn't fit into the overall structure of the American story.

Shays and Winstanley have a lot in common. Both were able to see that the countryside would not fare well when the creation of policy came to reside almost totally in the hands of commercial interests. Despite some obvious differences between them—Shays was clearly not a writer, he lacked Winstanley's ability to envision an alternative, and he decided, ultimately, that violence was an acceptable last resort in the pursuit of his vision for social justice—there are at least two similarities that unite the two men. First, they were both swiftly and violently taken to task for the threats they posed to the established order. And second, both were thereafter marginalized by historians who relegated their ideas, thoughts, and actions to the footnotes of our history texts.

There is nothing particularly wrong with this version of history if one is satisfied with the way things are in this country, as this version serves to legitimate the status quo for those who read it. It is worth taking a closer look at Shays' Rebellion, however, if you happen to live in the countryside and you are disillusioned by what is happening to your community. Far from being an unimportant footnote, what happened in rural New England in 1786 and 1787 represents the start of a trend regarding the fate of the countryside in America. It is much easier to begin to change the circumstances affecting one's community with an understanding of the historical forces aligned against success. Daniel Shays lacked such an understanding, but he nevertheless set out on an attempt to improve life's circumstances for his family, his neighbors, and his community. He found it rough going, to say the least.

The story began with the creation of what Szatmary calls the "chain of debt." Banned from trading with the British West Indies after the Revolution, American merchants found themselves dealing primarily with their former enemy directly. Many English wholesalers shipped large cargoes to American merchants on credit. By 1785, as America's trade deficit grew, English commercial firms began demanding the repayment of loans, and many of them stipulated that payment needed to be made in hard money (specie) rather than with raw materials or manufactured goods (tender).

In their turn, the seaboard shipping interests recalled their loans from inland merchants, who then passed the burden on to the local farmers. In each case, the demand was for specie payments, something extremely scarce in the countryside. Farmers all across New England called for legislation that would either infuse paper money into the economy or would officially sanction the payment of debts with tender (generally farm commodities such as grain or meat). Tender was not what the merchants wanted, however, and experiments with printing paper money during the Revolution had proved to be disastrous for merchants. Springfield, Massachusetts, businessman William Pynchon (descendant of the seventeenth-century patrician John Pynchon) claimed with others that paper money was "pregnent with innumerable evils, both political and moral . . . and inconsistent with the rights of mankind."[4]

Unable to pay their debts with specie, farmers were taken into debtor court at rapidly rising rates between 1784 and 1786. In some New England counties, the debtor toll was as high as one-third of all the adult males. To make matters worse, Massachusetts began demanding that taxes be paid with specie. The result was that law enforcement officials had no choice but to seize the property of debtors or to incarcerate them. By 1785, both options were vigorously employed.

Most of the farmers who found themselves landless or in jail were veterans of the recent American Revolution. Daniel Shays, for instance, was something of a war hero, having risen to the rank of captain. One can easily imagine the disillusionment of these men, confronted with such high rates of court-enforced dispossession. Was this what freedom was all about? Had they risked their lives in the war with England only to find themselves jailed for circumstances beyond their control?

It is not surprising that New England farmers banded together to try to put a stop to these developments. Szatmary estimates that as many as nine thousand militant farmers joined the multistate movement now known as Shays' Rebellion. Groups sometimes numbering in the hundreds would descend on debtor courts to break up the proceedings. On September 20, 1786, a group of angry farmers held the New Hampshire governor and Assembly captive for five hours. In all of these instances, the goal of Shays and other leaders was to put pressure on the states to pass legislation on paper money or tender in order to alleviate the tremendous burden on farmers. In the New England states, it was only in Rhode Island that the farmers were successful at this. Although it should be said that there were significant depreciation problems associated with this legislation in Rhode Island, the middle and southern states (specifically Pennsylvania, New York, New Jersey, and South Carolina) enacted similar laws without creating economic difficulties.

Throughout most of New England, seaboard merchants dug in their heels and vowed that they would not give in to the farmers' demands. When rumors began to circulate that England might send troops to come to the aid of the farmers, appeals were made to Henry Knox, the secretary of war under the Confederation, to bring out a national militia to put down the rebellion. Knox was able to convince the Confederation Congress to appropriate $530,000 for a national army created to suppress the farmer insurgents. To avoid public outcry, Congress called for the troops under the pretext of dealing with Indian troubles. Much to the dismay of the seaboard commercial interests in New England, however, most of the states in the Confederation rejected payment of their share of the $530,000. Undaunted, Massachusetts merchants pooled their own money and funded a militia force of their own, armed to the hilt, directed to defeat the rebel farmers.

On January 27, 1787, the merchants' army met a group of about 1,200 farmers at Springfield, Massachusetts. Lining up their cannons, the militia sent several volleys of grapeshot into the ranks of the farmers. In the aftermath, four farmers lay dead, many were injured, and the rest dispersed into the countryside. Thereafter, the rebels resorted to small, covert attacks on the homes and businesses of those who had made the most egregious demands on small farmers. In the end, many leaders were rounded up and put behind bars, although some, like Shays, were able to escape this fate by moving out of the state of Massachusetts. As with the diggers in England, the farmers of New England were swiftly punished for their attempt to demand equitable treatment from the "great men," as the Shaysites often referred to them, who had gained control of economic policy in the newly formed state governments.

As many diggers had done, several Shaysites wrote open letters to the public from their jail cells. Those documents that have survived tell a story somewhat different from the one that comes through in school history books. Szatmary related the following story:

> A Hampshire County farmer wrote that he had "labored hard all" his days and "fared hard," and had "been obliged to do more than my part in the war." Yet he had been "loaded with class-rates, lawsuits, and had [his] cattle sold for less than they were worth." "Great men," he feared, were "going to get all that we have" and reduce independent farmers to peonage.[5]

Another farmer wrote, "I had no intention to destroy the public government, but to have the courts suspended to prevent such abuses as have taken place by the sitting of these courts, distressed to see valuable members of society dragged from their families to prison."[6]

By contrast, the authors of a recent U.S. history textbook take one piece of data—the words of an outraged farmer—and attempt to cast the entire agrarian rebellion in an unfavorable light: "My boys, you are going to fight for liberty. If you wish to know what liberty is, I will tell you. It is for every man to do as he pleases, to make others do as you please to have them, and to keep folks from serving the devil."[7]

The textbook authors use this isolated quotation to introduce a concept that they apparently feel all Americans must learn to abhor: "For many citizens such words were a prescription for *anarchy*. Anarchy is the complete disorder that can result from having no government or laws."[8] Here, the suggestion is that all of the thousands of farmers who participated in the revolt were fundamentally antigovernment and, further, since this view is so self-evidently ignorant, if not malicious, that quick repression of the farmers ought to be seen as a contribution to our national greatness. Although most textbooks are not quite so blatant in their attempt to mislead young American citizens, it remains true nevertheless that the opportunity for a thorough investigation of Shays' Rebellion is denied most public-school students. Because the episode is symbolic of the subordination of rural interests to the power of urban commercial interests in this country, it is especially onerous that rural schoolchildren are not permitted to sort through the connections between this incident and the circumstances that currently touch their lives.

Those connections are many and powerful. For instance, calls for a constitutional convention multiplied rapidly during peak periods of Shaysite activity. The agrarian rebellion was a source of tremendous anxiety and insecurity among traders and merchants. They repeatedly asked for the creation of a strong central government, one with the power to stabilize what they took to be an altogether too volatile social and economic scene. For many, the failure of the Confederation to come up with a military force to put down the rebel farmers was the last straw. The convention opened in Philadelphia during summer 1787, just months after Shaysite resistance was finally dispersed.

The Philadelphia convention produced the Constitution that still orchestrates the political affairs of our nation. Although students in school are often asked when the convention was called and when the Constitution was ratified, they are seldom asked to study the context in which the convention was called or the content of the Constitution. It is worth a very brief look at both, however, to demonstrate what such inquiry might reveal and what the results of such inquiry might mean for rural students.

Szatmary does an admirable job of using historical data to illuminate the context surrounding the Constitutional Convention. One Massachusetts assemblyman complained that "the whole opposition, in this commonwealth, is that cursed spirit of insurgency that prevailed last year." Knox, the former Confederation secretary of war, attributed opposition to the Constitution "to the late insurgents, and all of those who abetted their designs." On the other side, an opponent of the Constitution claimed that it would throw "the whole power of the federal government into the hands of those who are in the mercantile interest." Still another farmer maintained that the Constitution would "get all the power and all the money into the hands of lawyers and men of learning, and monied men." As the Constitution neared ratification, still another claimed that "the liberties of the yeomanry are at an end."[9]

Thomas Jefferson can be added to the ranks of agrarian opposition to the Constitution: "I confess there are things in it which stagger all my dispositions to subscribe to what such an assembly has proposed," he wrote to John Adams from his ambassador's post in Paris. A few weeks after that, he confided to James Madison: "I own I am not a friend to very energetic government. It is always oppressive. The late rebellion in Massachusetts has given more alarm than I think it should have done."[10] It was almost more than Jefferson could take to be sitting in Paris while his countrymen were creating a new government.

Although admitting that there were problems with the Confederation, Jefferson did not like what he perceived to be the replacement of popular sovereignty with Lockean-inspired constitutional sovereignty. In other words, he did not like removing the burden of solving public disputes from the people and assigning it to various constitutional mechanisms:

And say, finally, whether peace is best preserved by giving energy to the government, or information to the people. The last is the most certain, and the most legitimate engine of government. Educate and inform the whole mass of people. Enable them to see that it is their interest to preserve peace and order, and they will preserve them ... they are the only sure reliance for the preservation of our liberty.

As Daniel Kemmis has pointed out, Jefferson is speaking of education for citizenship, "the heart of which was to enable people to see (and then act upon) the common good."[11]

There is a noticeable similarity between the educational ideas that came to Jefferson, given his take on political and economic questions, and those that Gerrard Winstanley espoused, given his vision for a democratic agrarian republic.[12] Both saw a kind of democratic surveillance over policy creation as a necessary end result of education, a viewpoint that has been dropped totally from the rhetoric of school reform these days in favor of marshaling our educational power to improve American odds in the international economic competition.

The important point to keep in mind is that Jefferson and other rural opponents of the Constitution looked upon the transfer of dispute settlement from the hands of the people to the hands of the government as a serious blow to democracy. But this didn't trouble the likes of John Jay, Alexander Hamilton, and James Madison, authors of *The Federalist Papers*. As noted in Chapter 1, they believed that people were not capable of settling their own disputes and that it was the proper role of government to do this for them. Harvard University political scientist Michael Sandel maintains that the Constitution set in motion "the procedural republic." Not only would such a republic settle disputes between the people for the people, but it would also effectively generate policy that would preserve the common interest, not by handing it to the whims of the masses but by unfettering individual volition in the marketplace. Adam Smith's invisible hand, in other words, was hard at work by the time the constitutional architects assembled in Philadelphia. Democracy, in the sense that all people should have a voice in the decisions that affect their lives or even in the weaker sense that all should have a vote, was not feasible political theory according to the Philadelphia delegates. Property would dictate how far democracy would extend in the United States.

Connecticut patriot and businessman Noah Webster clearly made this distinction. In the textbooks he published for the children of the new nation, he warned of the evils not only of a monarchy but also of a democracy. He believed he had witnessed such evils firsthand in the jaded agenda of the Shaysite rebels. He chastised the farmers by claiming that contracts are "sacred things" and that the "right of property is a sacred right."[13] The intent of such emotionally charged rhetoric was obvious. Property was to be the basis for operationalizing subsequent economic and political policy in this country.

Although the story continues, we should pause here long enough to acknowledge the way in which history and philosophy came together so vividly in Philadelphia during summer 1787. Any vestiges of liberal thought akin to the ideas of Winstanley—and here we could perhaps count such agrarian spokespersons as Dickinson, Crevecoeur, and Jefferson (but also thousands of small farmers and artisans all across the country)—was summarily dismissed. A deliberate choice was made, and it should be becoming clear to the reader that this choice structured in the domination of urban over rural concerns.

Daniel M. Friedenberg, in his provocative account of early American history entitled *Life, Liberty, and the Pursuit of Land*, contends in his conclusion that

> the pre-Revolutionary colonial system, which openly operated for the benefit of the British aristocracy and its hirelings, had been recast to a significant extent, though in modified form, for the benefit of the post-colonial upper class. The structure set up in this crucial period—from the Revolution to the election of Thomas Jefferson as president—became a prototype for government in the emerging republic, whose techniques still remain with us in one distorted fashion or another.[14]

Friedenberg describes how the small farmers who formed the rank and file of the revolutionary army received scrip that allotted them western lands but were later forced to sell these properties to speculators for whatever cash they could get for them. But in order for these speculators (many of whom became U.S. congressmen) to profit, the removal of Indians was first required, something it didn't look like the Confederation, given the Shays debacle, had the ability to do. This provided one more reason, according to Friedenberg, to hold the Constitutional Convention and institute the procedures it put in place. As Freidenberg remarked, "What seemed like checks and balances was in effect a narrow corset of monied privilege at times trussed by corruption."[15]

*   *   *

There is more evidence from early American history. Just a few years after the Constitution was ratified, another farmer rebellion was in the making. This one came about in response to Alexander Hamilton's tax levied on alcoholic beverages in 1791. The tax affected most western farmers between Georgia and Pennsylvania, for those in the far reaches of these states had found it most profitable to convert the grain they raised into strong drink before transporting it to western cities or the eastern seaboard. Because of the nature of the commodity in question, it has been doubly easy for historians to chastise as "rioters" and "bullies" those farmers involved in what has come to be known as the Whiskey Rebellion.[16]

Matters came to a head during summer 1794. Farmers in four western Pennsylvania counties began to obstruct the work of revenue collectors, and like the Shaysites before them, they frequently stopped court proceedings. Rumors even circulated about a march on Pittsburgh. President George Washington had his opportunity to demonstrate how the new centralized government could respond in ways the old Confederation could not. A militia of 12,900 men was called up and placed under the command of General Henry Lee. After inspection by the president himself, the troops marched into western Pennsylvania. Not surprisingly, the farmers were in no mood to clash with such a huge, well-armed force. Lee's soldiers were forced to chase up and down the countryside in search of individuals who might be dubbed leaders of the insurrection. At last they returned to Philadelphia with twenty ragged prisoners. Two were eventually charged with treason but were later pardoned by Washington because one was a "simpleton" and the other was "insane."

The fiasco was deemed a great show of strength by Hamilton and his federalist colleagues. Jefferson referred to it as the rebellion that "could never be found." To the farmers, it was further evidence that the new republic was dedicated to the advance of commercialist interests at the expense, if necessary, of the nation's rural yeomanry.

As the eighteenth century gave way to the nineteenth, other examples of the primacy of commercialist interests surfaced. The rocky, hilly terrain in New England had always meant that agricultural production was destined to be a tenuous affair. Free access to Atlantic salmon, shad, and other anadromous fish that spawned annually in the upper reaches of area rivers was important; these fish were a significant source of protein in the diet of local farmers and served as a barter and exchange staple in local economies. As industrialists moved in to tap the waterpower in these areas, they constructed dams that not only obstructed the free passage of fish but also caused severe flooding problems for low-lying farms. Although farmers fought the construction of these dams with petitions and lawsuits, and on at least two occasions with hammers and axes, the desires of blast furnace owners and, later, cotton millers took precedence in legislation concerning water and property rights. Recognizing the inequity of these developments, Henry David Thoreau wrote in 1839, "Who knows what may avail a crow bar against that . . . dam."[17]

*   *   *

It is useful, I believe, to take a look at the careers of Thoreau and his mentor-colleague, Ralph Waldo Emerson, two of the most accomplished essayists in American history. Throughout the middle years of the nineteenth century, they watched a nation in transition. America, in fact, was moving west. The West was a viable option for many, whether they were Massachusetts farmers who lost their land in debtor courts or their counterparts in Pennsylvania who went broke as a result of the whiskey tax, the second or third sons of small farmers with no chance at a viable inheritance in land, agricultural laborers never able to acquire a deed to land of their own, or victims of any one of the innumerable exigencies that made obtaining and maintaining a farm in one of the original thirteen states a difficult proposition.

Americans spoke of "manifest destiny," and some openly embraced genocide with regard to the native inhabitants of the continent. After all, as many were given to say, "The only good Indian is a dead Indian." Chattel slavery spread as far as the western portions of Texas, Arkansas, and Missouri. It was an acquisitive time, and it was hard on many population groups, including women, as Wendell Berry observed:

> I don't know how exact a case can be made, but it seems to me that there is an historical parallel, in white American history, between the treatment of the land and the treatment of women. The frontier, for instance, was notoriously exploitive of both, and I believe largely for the same reasons. Many of the early farmers seem to have worn out farms and wives with equal regardlessness, interested in both mainly for what they would produce, crops and dollars, labor and sons; they clambered upon their fields and upon their wives, struggling for an economic foothold.[18]

Industries grew up and were linked by proliferating rail lines. The seamy side of urban industries appeared almost overnight. Thoreau and Emerson distinguished themselves as opponents of the sort of hyperpossessive culture in the making. Both believed that it was in the farming life that mankind's best propensities were developed. Working with nature and providing sustenance for fellow human beings were circumstances afforded to the farmer that enabled him to work for moral rather than pecuniary ends.[19] And, according to Emerson, "the moral influence of nature upon every individual is that amount of truth which it illustrates to him."[20] Thus farming, by bringing humans nearer to the truth, provided an enhanced opportunity for them to lead deeper, more fulfilling lives. Of course, this was the very reason that Thoreau settled and planted his beans at Walden Pond. And for his part, Emerson at one time contemplated participating in the agrarian schemes that he and Thoreau had, in part, inspired. These included the experiment in agrarian self-sufficiency at Brook Farm and the colony created by their friend and literary colleague, Bronson Alcott, called Fruitlands.

Perhaps it is possible to get a better understanding of what Thoreau and Emerson were "transcending" as leading spokespersons of what came to be known as the transcendentalist movement—a loose collection of nineteenth-century Americans who tried to live simply, by inspiration, and in harmony with nature's laws—if we review certain circumstances in the larger early American political economy. Born as the country was during the Enlightenment, mechanisms used to check "regal power" were employed here in great measure. One such mechanism was institution building. Associations of manufacturers, guilds, commerce groups, stock companies, boards of trade, and the like were all created to facilitate political and economic change to the advantage of those seeking power. The early national period in our history was marked by a plethora of institution building, whether it was Henry Clay striving to create a commercial infrastructure of roads, canals, and bridges; Horace Bushnell calling for a system of playgrounds and city parks; Catharine Beecher building a following to advocate temperance and Sunday schools; or Horace Mann drawing up plans for tax-supported common schools. The rationalism of the Enlightenment suggested that American character and values needed to be institutionalized. As Benjamin Rush once wrote, "I consider it as possible to convert men into republican machines." Viewing circumstances in America during the early 1830s, Alexis de Tocqueville commented that "in every case, at the head of any new undertaking, where in France you would find the government or in England some territorial magnate, in the United States you are sure to find an Association."[21]

Thoreau and Emerson sought to transcend this emphasis on perfecting human institutions predicated in Enlightenment thought and to get on with the business of perfecting individuals. To this end, they did not look with much favor on Mann's system of schooling, a system that seemed to have a great deal to suggest itself to the industrialist and not nearly so much, however, to someone concerned with learning. Said Thoreau:

How vain to try to teach youth, or anybody else, truths! They can only learn them after their own fashion, and when they get ready. I do not mean by this to condemn our system of education, but to show what it amounts to . . . they get a valuable drilling, it *may* be, but they do not learn what you profess to teach [Thoreau's emphasis].[22]

For his part, Mann was not willing to recognize that the agrarian life was closely tied to nature and subsequently to truths of any sort. Probably reacting as much to the Swing Riots in England as to anything else, Mann, ever the proponent of industrial interests, maintained that

agrarianism is the revenge of poverty against wealth. The wanton destruction of the property of others—the burning of hay-ricks and corn-ricks, the demolition of machinery, because it supersedes hand labor, the sprinkling of vitriol on rich dresses—is only agrarianism run mad. Education prevents both the revenge and the madness.[23]

In his words it is possible to see the industrialist's emphasis on property rights that so often accompanies a general unwillingness to discuss questions concerning human rights. Furthermore, the hopes of industrialists rested on the common schools of the country—to produce future scientists who could refine technological capital as well as a stable, compliant force of human capital. As education historians have pointed out, the American system of common schools was largely a response to urban, industrial problems.[24] As such, the system has been imbued with industrial tenets like specialization, competition, efficiency, and so forth. Efforts to pass these tenets on to rural schools met with a great amount of local resistance. Rural schools seemingly substituted some agrarian tenets when they were finally forced to adopt the common school concept.[25]

Emerson wrote indirectly about a few of these agrarian tenets. For him, the increasingly industrial political economy led to a kind of consumerism that foreshadowed Thorstein Veblen's notion of "conspicuous consumption." Referring to his own spending habits, Emerson lamented that

custom does it for me, gives me no power therefrom, and runs me into debt to boot. We spend our incomes for paint and paper, for a hundred trifles, I know not what, and not for the things of a man. Our expense is almost all for conformity. It is for cake that we run in debt; it is not for the intellect, not the heart, not beauty, not worship, that costs so much.[26]

The farmer, on the other hand, acquires only in proportion to the dictates of Nature: "His entertainments, his liberties and his spending must be on a farmer's scale." Emerson maintained that it is the farmer's part in the "great

Economy," that is, Nature, to operate in "small economies" in his relations with others.[27] For Emerson, the farmer who exercises autonomy over his consumption is the truly free individual. The agrarian thought of both Emerson and Thoreau is first concerned with a positive conception of human freedom, a conception reminiscent of Gerrard Winstanley. The communion with nature, the conscientious consumption manifest in Emerson's "mid-world"—these things suggest a moral tie to the farming life.

I digressed from the story of America's nineteenth-century rural history long enough to consider the work of Emerson and Thoreau because it is important to demonstrate that there has been much more than what is often perceived pejoratively as "nostalgia" at work behind the claim that farming is more than a business. Although many who try to defend this position may not be aware of it, there is a weighty scholarly tradition undergirding it, which we shall pick up again in the next chapter. For now, I'd simply like to add that in addition to that of Thoreau and Emerson, one could include the work of John Burroughs, John Muir, Peter Kropotkin, Albert Howard, Liberty Hyde Bailey, Lewis Mumford, E. F. Schumacher, Aldo Leopold, David Orr, Wes Jackson, Marty Strange, and Wendell Berry in this tradition. Sorting through this body of work, judging its merits, considering alternatives, and so on should be a part of the school curriculum for every rural child.

*   *   *

What was life like for the average American during this age of acquisition, this expansion of nineteenth-century America? There is a tendency to assume that because a vast frontier was opened, everyone who wanted land in this country was able to acquire it. Not only this, but there is also a tendency to assume that since there was so much land, people often settled in one place only to discover that the grass looked greener elsewhere or that the smoke from the chimney of the nearest neighbor was too close, and so people moved to another place, on little more than the basis of a whim.

Recent historical research does not bear out these assumptions. In fact, the tremendous rates of mobility that marked the history of the interior Plains States turn out to have been the result of people engaged in a difficult quest for landownership. We incorrectly interpret the frontier experience if we refer to the West as an "opportunity." It was an alternative, certainly, but not an attractive one by any means. Evidence indicates that those who "went west searching for land could expect to live in a single-room dwelling with an average of six other persons, could expect to have to hew down huge trees and grub out stumps to create fields to grow crops, could expect to go without churches and schools for extended periods, could expect to walk great distances to visit neighbors or to wash clothes in a stream or to bring back water for household and livestock."[28] The question ought to be this: Why did so many people subject themselves to this kind of hardship?

The answer is that western pioneers were seeking propertied status; that is, they wished more than anything to be able to own their own land. Prior to their arrival, the U.S. government had skillfully platted the interior through surveys. It was divided into 640-acre squares with the express purpose of easing the sale of these lands to the benefit of the federal government and, as Daniel Friedenberg has demonstrated, certain congressmen and legislators. Many of the well-positioned were able to make fortunes as a result of federal land sales in the West, and many more made (and sometimes lost) fortunes through townsite speculation. The vast majority of those who went west, however, did so because they had been effectively denied access to propertied status in the East (or in Europe, in the case of immigrant farmers). In the interior, they were hoping that things would be different.

A number of studies show clearly now that acquiring land in one of the seaboard states prior to 1800 was a difficult proposition.[29] Often boys would "hire out" as agricultural laborers in the vicinity of home until their father passed away. If there was more than one son, the home place was sometimes sold and the proceeds divided among the sons, who then went west, where land was cheaper and the odds of acquiring a farm with the divided inheritance proceeds were better.[30] Sometimes sons ended up with little or nothing and lived out their lives as agricultural laborers or tenant farmers. As Henretta has shown, in eighteenth-century New England, "propertied status was the product of one or two decades of work as a laborer or tenant, or of the long-delayed inheritance of the parental farm. The ownership of a freehold estate may have been the goal of young male farmers; it was not, even in the best of circumstances, a universal condition among adult males at any time." As a result, Henretta contends, "there was a steady increase in the number of permanent tenant farmers as the century progressed."[31] Given these circumstances, it is easier to see how people could decide that moving west, despite the enormous difficulties and hardships it entailed, was their best shot at successfully coming to own land.

After the turn of the century and especially after the War of 1812, people moved into the interior plains region at unprecedented rates. For instance, there were thirteen thousand people in Illinois before federal land sales began there in 1814.[32] During the first generation of settlement in these areas, the rates of landlessness dipped below what they were east of the Appalachians, but it did not take long for the "class of agricultural laborers and tenants" to become as predictable a part of the midwestern scene as it was in older regions of the North. As Peter C. Mancall has maintained, "In the rapidly expanding agricultural West, farm tenancy and wage labor emerged shortly after the initial settlement of the region. Few pioneers were able to climb the economic ladder to become property holders." Most of the early thirteen thousand "squatters," as they came to be called, "became farm laborers or tenants or they moved on, seeking an independent life in a wilderness that proved ever elusive."[33]

The work of historian John Mack Faragher dealing with the first few generations of settlement in Illinois confirms Mancall's observations. In the Sugar Creek vicinity that Faragher studied, there were two groups, "a majority with high levels of mobility, who farmed for a time before pushing on, and a significantly more permanent landed minority who rooted themselves in the community during the first decades of settlement, first established the neighborhoods, then lived and worked together in them for many years, intermarrying and passing their improved farms on to their children."[34] Henretta's analysis also concurs: "Within a few decades of settlement the wealth structure of the frontier states was nearly indistinguishable from that in the agricultural areas of the more densely settled East."[35] Farm tenancy was the rule, not the exception.

Many of those who ceaselessly moved found themselves on the arid plains of the trans-Mississippi West. There they sometimes constructed their soddies, homes that were little more than holes in the ground. Pushed to the very limits of territory suitable for rainfall agriculture, many of those whose lives had been defined by mobility said simply, "No further." Here they would make a stand and demand equitable treatment from the railroad corporations, the implement companies, the warehouse interests, the insurance houses, and the rest who were making profits at the expense of their livelihoods. The last consequential agrarian protest movement in the nation's history would emanate from these dry states and the troubled farmers who had come there to acquire land of their own; but their story will be told in the next chapter.

There is another history that has come from the plains. It is the history of the propertied minority, those who were successful in their pursuit of land. There is much that is eminently laudable in their story. They worked hard. They built and controlled schools and churches. They orchestrated community work "bees" and community celebrations. In short, their views and their actions came to define the character of local communities as well as the direction these communities took. Faragher contends that community was, in fact, the vehicle that "assured the success of the persistent [the propertied minority] and the continuity of their culture amid the flux of change."[36] There were exclusionary dimensions to rural communities across the interior plains, as anyone who has moved as an outsider into one of these places can attest. The reasons for this exclusionary dimension go back to our feudal past, but all the same, it cannot be condoned by any reasonable person. Those who are committed to charting a course that leads to rural community revitalization should recognize the educative power of the local school for its potential to subdue some of the less ennobling forces that sometimes lurk within rural communities.

* * *

It may be worthwhile at this point to summarize some of the historical terrain covered in Chapters 4 and 5 and in the process create a useful introduction to Chapter 6.

Recall that at the very moment feudalism was crushed in England, Thomas Hobbes and Gerrard Winstanley offered well-argued, albeit fundamentally different, blueprints for England's future. Winstanley's vision was grounded in what was best in agrarian feudal traditions. These were to be undergirded by a lifelong educational system that nurtured community allegiance and its attendant propensity for democratic surveillance of political and economic decisionmaking. Hobbes' vision was grounded in emerging commercialist traditions. These were to be undergirded by a strong centralized state and nurtured by an educational system intent on maximizing an individual's competitive impulses.

When the United States was created, both of these visions existed side by side. The fallout over Shays' Rebellion in Massachusetts, however, tipped the scales in favor of the Hobbesian vision. In due course, the American interior was opened, and as that occurred, a frantic scramble for the acquisition of property began. Even the churches took part in an extremely divisive competition for souls in the interior, the first large-scale experiment in the separation of church and state. A close look at rural history in the United States demonstrates, however, that the importance of communal ties and traditions remained strong despite the larger acquisitive, competitive milieu, exhibited in bold talk of the nation's "manifest destiny."

This allegiance to cooperative communal traditions eventually consolidated in what has become known as the Populist movement of the 1890s, but that is a subject for the next chapter. Before moving on to that, however, it should be noted that other Western countries, most notably Denmark and Sweden, opted to follow an agrarian liberal trajectory closely aligned to Winstanley's vision. The end result was not poverty and isolation but vigorous, globally competitive industrial production flanked by the healthiest rural communities on earth. Nonetheless, since the 1980s, with the ascendancy of multinational corporations to positions that supersede national or international sanction, the countryside in these places has suffered severely.

It was the long public career of Nikolaj Frederik Grundtvig (1783–1872), a Lutheran minister from Denmark, that solidified this Winstanleyan agrarian trajectory. The author of hundreds of poems, thousands of hymns, and countless essays and sermons, Grundtvig became the clear spokesperson for

Danish identity, although he enjoyed a wide following in Sweden as well. The end result of these countries' embrace of Grundtvig's ideas was that both of them formed national identities without engaging in the fiercely competitive chauvinism of the political decisionmakers in most Western countries. Grundtvig captured the wisdom of traditional peasant feeling for community and used it to repel the modern liberal emphasis on creating competitive selves. And in the process he proved that such a mentality is not by nature inimical to industrialization.

Grundtvig's most pronounced impact resulted from the part he played in the creation of two Danish institutions: the cooperative movement in agriculture and the "folk school" concept. In agriculture, Danish farmers came together to create cooperative processing enterprises that would convert farm products into exportable commodities. The success of these arrangements, along with the spirit of community that seemed to emanate from them, constrained Danish political institutions from acting in ways that might have been detrimental to the countryside.

The other contribution that served to guarantee this end was Grundtvig's educational agenda. He was an advocate of practical learning bolstered by extensive discussion and deliberation among peers. He worked to create many agrarian schools for the sons and daughters of farmers, as well as the still-legendary folk high schools. In folk schools, students studied local culture in the form of stories, myths, sagas, and other literary forms. The idea was to nurture the best of Denmark's peasant traditions and to simultaneously produce a sense of community allegiance and political efficacy. Even the state-sponsored Danish schools today are heavily influenced by their larger cooperative culture. In fact, some Danish parents living just north of the German border choose to send their children to German high schools so they might learn to become more competitive.[37]

The late nineteenth-century cooperative movements across the American countryside owe a great deal to Grundtvig and the Scandinavians who fleshed out the concept. But the American embrace of cooperative institutions took place at a very inopportune moment; that is, the farmer cooperatives appeared at the tail end of the period of acquisition in this country and at the beginning of the period of dispossession. The next chapter demonstrates just how bad this timing was.

6

The American Countryside and the Dynamics of Dispossession

Environmental degradation and the decay in our concept of citizenship occurred simultaneously and as mutually reinforcing trends.
—David Orr, 1992

In 1893, the since-famous historian Frederick Jackson Turner announced that the frontier was closed. There were no more vacant lands of consequence to which one might go with the intention of making a living. The interior had filled, and the near century-long drive for the acquisition of land was effectively halted. A new period of rural history was beginning, a period characterized by the very opposite of acquisition.

As the previous chapters have demonstrated, however, dispossession was a central part of the story of acquisition. One could point to the victims of English enclosure, to the followers of Daniel Shays in western Massachusetts who were without the specie required to pay their taxes, or to those who gradually joined the permanent agricultural laborer or tenant class across the Northeast and Midwest, or perhaps most poignantly, to those native inhabitants who were brutally pushed aside in the name of Christian expansion. Dispossession was the fate of them all, and the material in this chapter cannot be properly understood without an appreciation of this circumstance. Still, after 1893, the "unsettling" of the nation began at a dramatic pace.[1] The central feature of our history ceased to be mass attempts at the acquisition of land and became mass departure from the land.

Only decades earlier, Thomas Jefferson had believed that he had acquired enough land with the Louisiana Purchase for countless generations of small-scale freeholders. To put it mildly, he was wide of the mark, and with hindsight, we can easily see a certain predictability to the error in his estimation. The Locke-inspired sense of possessive individualism, the laissez-faire Enlightenment political theory, the Smithian self-interest economic theory, and the Protestant work ethic all added up to a feverish spirit of acquisition. Within such a milieu, it only makes sense that the countryside filled quickly.

The last places to fill were agricultural areas of the trans-Mississippi West. The lure of mining operations helped to people the rugged areas of the West. On the great arid plains of the Dakotas, Nebraska, Kansas, Oklahoma, Texas, eastern Colorado, eastern Wyoming, and eastern Montana, however, settlers excluded from settlement elsewhere stopped to make one last attempt to acquire a freeholding, albeit in a dry, difficult country. Some were aided in this attempt by homestead legislation passed in 1862. The Homestead Act is itself an interesting commentary on the treatment the United States has afforded those who live in the countryside. It is particularly interesting to take note of the timing involved. Recall that scrip for land was used by the revolutionary generation to keep a fighting army in the field. The promise of free land was perhaps the only thing that could have accomplished this. Although the call for free land coming out of the Midwest had been around for decades, it was not until 1862, when things were going badly for the Union army and when there was a great deal of resistance to conscription all across the North, that this legislation finally came into being. The promise of free land had a certain utility at a time when few northerners could identify with the causes undergirding the war.

By the time the system for giving away this land was put into place, however, the only lands available in any significant amount were in the states of the trans-Mississippi West. Most homesteading, in fact, took place in Minnesota, the Dakotas, and Nebraska. Even on the Great Plains, however, speculators found ways to use the law to acquire large holdings. Stories are still told in these states about parents who wrote "21" on the bottoms of their children's shoes. This allowed them to truthfully swear that they were "over 21" when they filed their claim. Also, reportedly, scores of cardboard houses measuring 14 x 16 inches were constructed in order to be able to truthfully say that a "14 x 16 board house" had been built on the homestead property when it came time to acquire the title.

Despite these abuses, thousands of families gained title to a viable farm, a circumstance that likely would have eluded most of them had it not been for the Homestead Act. The greatest gift of free land, however, went not to farmers but to railway entrepreneurs, as we shall shortly see. In any event, within a decade or two, the farmers who created farms out of the hard, dry prairie banded together to create an agrarian movement, the ramifications of which are little understood today. Before describing these, however, it is useful to examine some of the conditions that led to this movement.

After every war in which the United States became significantly involved, monetary policy became a question of utmost importance. War brings a flurry of financial activity, huge loans are made, productive energy is mobilized on a mass scale, and buying and selling goes on at a furious pace. When the war is over, things slow down considerably. How much money should be allowed to flow through the economy thereafter becomes a burning question. For the poor or for those in debt, maintaining high wartime levels is most beneficial. For the rich or for those who make money extending credit, reducing wartime levels is most beneficial. We saw this in the last chapter when at the conclusion of the Revolutionary War, farmers demanded the printing of paper money, as had been done during the war years, to help enable them to pay their debts and their taxes. The commercial interests that controlled public policy, however, refused. They chose a monetary policy that was most beneficial to themselves and refused to print paper money or even to accept tender payment on taxes.

The story that unfolded after the American Civil War was essentially the same, though the stakes in terms of the number of lives and livelihoods that hinged on monetary policy had risen dramatically. Just as it had during the Revolutionary War, during the Civil War the treasury department suspended specie payments and issued paper money in an attempt to facilitate the massive spending required to conduct the war. When the economy slowed as hostilities ceased, commercial interests once again called for the return to the specie standard. This required reducing, significantly, the amount of money flowing through the economy.

The effect of this is painfully clear. Debtor farmers in Dakota Territory would be paying back loans with dollars worth far more than those they had originally borrowed. Creditors, by contrast, would be receiving payment in dollars worth far more than those they originally loaned. It is not difficult to see that this monetary policy, like the one steadfastly embraced in postrevolutionary Massachusetts, was fundamentally detrimental to the interests of those living in the countryside. Because of the timing of the Civil War itself, as well as the timing inherent in the method chosen for reducing the money supply, the farmers of the trans-Mississippi West were destined to suffer the most egregious ramifications of these circumstances. Rather than immediately withdrawing money from the economy, postwar policymakers decided to keep the amount of money constant while the country expanded. In other words, rather than creating a seriously painful situation all at once, it was decided that the best course was to create more moderately painful circumstances and to extend them over time.

Monetary policy is often touted to be hopelessly complex, something certainly beyond the ken of average citizens. There can be no denying the obvious utility of this cultural message for those with the power to create monetary policy. In fact, elevating the need for "experts" in all facets of American decisionmaking became a deliberate policy in and of itself in the first years of the twentieth century, and this is something we will come back to later in this chapter. The historian Lawrence Goodwyn provides a clear picture of the post–Civil War monetary policy adopted in this country, and I will borrow his passage in order to demonstrate how easily this can be understood:

> Letting ten farmers symbolize the entire population, and ten dollars the entire money supply, and ten bushels of wheat the entire production of the economy, it is at once evident that a bushel of wheat would sell for one dollar. Should the population, production, and money supply increase to twenty over a period of, say, two generations, the farmers' return would still be one dollar per bushel. But should the population and production double to twenty while the money supply was held to ten—[a condition called] currency contraction—the price of wheat would drop to fifty cents. The farmers of the nation would get no more for twenty bushels of wheat than they had previously received for ten. Moreover, money being more scarce, interest rates would have risen considerably. A person who borrowed $1000 to buy a farm in 1868 would not only have to grow twice as much wheat in 1888 to earn the same mortgage payment he made earlier, he would be repaying his loan in dollars that had twice as much purchasing power as the depreciated currency he had originally borrowed. Thus, while contraction was a blessing to banker-creditors, it placed a cruel and exploitive burden on the nation's producer-debtors.[2]

The obvious lesson in these circumstances is that the concerns of rural dwellers were placed below the concerns of business interests. One might legitimately ask why this happened, why the slow return to the "gold standard" was the chosen policy when it was demonstrably detrimental to rural dwellers, who made up roughly three-fourths of the population.

The answer is that business interests couched their arguments in moral terms. The money supply needed "intrinsic value," they claimed, something gold ostensibly possessed. Anything less than "hard money" represented, for its advocates, a national character flaw. It is amazing, in retrospect, that an argument as shallow as this was used to win a policy victory that worked to the benefit of so few. It should be said, however, that the pain this policy caused depended very much on a person's level of debt. The farmers of the older, more established rural states suffered far less than those in the newer states of the trans-Mississippi West. Still, all of the talk about national moral integrity related to money of intrinsic value seemed to be just a smoke screen to the farmers of the country, established or not. At various times and in various places, farmers had lived through days when such items as salt or whiskey were used as money. The necessity for gold money was an empty argument. Far from being a question of morality, the nation's monetary policy was seen by late nineteenth-century rural dwellers as a question of power manipulated in the interest of greed.

* * *

The issue of postwar monetary policy represents one more lens through which we can view, historically, the inequitable treatment afforded the countryside. But this discussion also helps to set the context for our next topic, the agrarian revolt of the 1880s and 1890s. To move into this discussion, however, it is necessary to take a look at certain developments in the postwar rural South. Up to this point I have avoided direct discussion of these circumstances, for southern history is entwined with the story of human bondage and this has had a bearing on all developments within that region. After the Civil War, however, black and white farmers found themselves engulfed together in a postwar development that emerged as the "crop-lien" system. Barring slavery itself, there likely has never been a more demeaning, damnable existence afforded those who worked the land than the circumstances surrounding the orchestration of this system.

At the center of the crop-lien system was the "furnishing merchant," the man who supplied former slaves and poor whites with the food supplies, clothing, medicine, farm equipment, and seed required for a cotton-growing season. All of these items were extended on credit at a price that was near double the cash price and at interest rates that were frequently as high as 33 percent. Each year, of course, the farmers came out a little further in debt to the furnishing merchant. No matter how good their cotton crop was, they never seemed to earn enough to pay the exorbitant prices charged by the merchant. It was a trap from which no one seemed able to escape. A move to Texas frequently loomed as the only option out.

Goodwyn contends that the victims of the southern crop-lien system frequently needed to write no more than "G.T.T." on the door of their shack when they decided to make the move. All who came by thereafter would know that another family had "gone to Texas." Throughout the 1870s, one hundred thousand farmers straggled across the Sabine River each year looking for a chance to own their own land.[3] Although southern "push" factors were more overt and more egregiously exploitive, the northern states and territories like Kansas, Nebraska, and Dakota received hundreds of thousands of eager potential landowners as well. Most of those who went to these places did so because their chances of acquiring land back East (or back in Europe) were slim or nonexistent.

It is sometimes said that wagons filled with families heading West were almost a part of the midwestern landscape. Census data tell an indisputable story in this regard. Only a small percentage of the residents in any farming neighborhood in, say, 1850, were still there in 1860. Those who stayed belonged to the "persistent families," as Faragher has called them, the minority of midwestern settlers who were actually able to acquire titles to their own farms. Traditionally, this ceaseless westward movement has been interpreted either as steadfast speculation (a seemingly insatiable drive among many to buy cheap land ahead of heavy settlement and sell it at high prices later) or as a uniquely American propensity to adhere to the belief that the grass is always greener over the next hill.

The recent work of rural historians like Faragher and Henretta raises serious questions about these interpretations, to say the least. In any case, who could reason that the grass would be greener in such dry places as Nebraska and the Dakotas? From Texas to North Dakota, the nation's last pioneers set out to purchase or homestead and thereafter to build productive farms of their own. There was no shortage of credit-extending institutions to help the migrants to the trans-Mississippi West. In Kansas, for instance, it has been estimated that during the late 1880s there was one mortgage for every two adults.[4] The deeply indebted farmers on the plains found themselves increasingly squeezed by the nation's policy of currency contraction. They suffered through extreme levels of deprivation and hardship. Many families lived for years in their sod houses. Countless district schools were similarly constructed. Times were extraordinarily difficult.

For a brief moment in history, the beleaguered, transient farmers in the North found a bit of common ground with the victims of the crop-lien system in the South. Together they created a mass movement calling for social justice and for an end to the impoverished circumstances that defined their lives. Their organization was the Farmers Alliance and it grew from a modest beginning in Texas into a massive national undertaking with suballiances in forty-three states. The movement culminated in the creation of a political party called the People's or Populist Party. It was one of the largest "third-party threats" (note the interesting connotation in this commonplace colloquialism) in American history.

The demise of the Populist moment is one of the saddest chapters of that history. Of course it doesn't read this way in the textbooks our children study, but from a rural perspective, it is nevertheless sad because it is obvious that the Populist movement was the last viable, forthright attempt by rural dwellers to put the country on an equitable course, on a trajectory that would attend to the interests of the producers as well as those of the commercial interests. There is a great deal of controversy surrounding the demise of this movement. A common account maintains that in the first decade of the new century, farmers received better prices for their produce and thereafter quit "bellyaching" and went back to farming. This, of course, is a hopelessly simplistic and shallow explanation. The demise of the Populist movement is convoluted, to be sure, but it is necessary to work through the details of this story because the commercialist response to it was the Progressive Era agenda, something that held dramatic ramifications for life in the countryside and for public schooling everywhere.

In the final analysis, the demise of the Populist movement may be tied directly to the initiatives it undertook to advance the social justice it stood for. Populism was indeed a threat to the established power structure in this country. It offered farmers genuine, viable alternatives to the credit-extending institutions, rail interests, insurance houses, grain buyers, millers, and warehouse interests that were seemingly gouging them at every turn. The men and women of the Farmers Alliance vowed to create a "cooperative commonwealth" that would have seriously challenged the wisdom ostensibly inherent in the individualistic competitive culture that gave birth to our feverish rush to acquire and consume. For a brief period, the spirit of Gerrard Winstanley was alive in the United States.

The tight money policies of the postwar government meant that all farmer purchases became more costly as each year went by. Struggling to pay their mortgages and to purchase needed implements, seeds, food, medicine, and clothing, farmers grew increasingly bitter about the tremendous wealth accruing in the hands of rail companies. For one thing, rail companies charged outrageous rates when it came to individual farmers but gave substantially reduced rates to other corporations. For instance, it cost a farmer more to ship grain from Mankato to Minneapolis within Minnesota than it did for Pillsbury to ship grain from Minneapolis out of state to Chicago. And not only this. Rail companies quickly got into the business of building elevators for grain storage next to their rail stations. If a farmer wanted to wait for a better price, he had to store the grain and pay the rail company for storage space. Further, farmers were all too aware of the fact that the nation's rail companies were the real winners in the national free land giveaway. In fact, all told, the federal government gave away 130 million acres of land to various rail companies between 1850 and 1871, or more territory than all of the states of New England plus New York and Pennsylvania combined. Additionally, nine state governments gave another 49 million acres to rail companies.[5] When the abuses perpetrated by speculators are factored into an accounting of land given by the federal government to farmers, the total pales in comparison to the incredible amounts of unearned wealth simply handed over to railroad businesses.

To the farmers of the trans-Mississippi West, this was evidence of the fact that the federal government was making a clear choice to support commercial enterprises at the expense of farmers. A Minnesota man, writing his congressman, complained:

> I settled on this land in good Faith Built House and Barn Broken up Part of the
> land. Spent years in hard labor in grubing fencing and Improving are they

going to drive us out like tresspassers wife and children give us away to corporations how we can support them. When we are robed of our means. they will shurely not stand this we must Decay or Die from Woe and Sorrow We are loyal citicens and do Not intend to intrude on any R.R. Corporation we Beleived and still do Beleive that the R.R. Co. has got no legal title to this land in question. We love our wife and children just as dearly as any of you But how can we protect them give them education as they should wen we are driven from sea to sea.[6]

Most likely, this individual ended up on land in the Dakotas and was quite likely a staunch Populist. Notice the fact that though he had obviously received very little schooling himself, education was something he wanted for his children. Indeed, the states of the trans-Mississippi West became the first to apply the standard of democracy to educational questions. Residents in these states lobbied their legislators for laws that would require school districts to purchase schoolbooks for all district children. According to the Mandan, North Dakota, *Pioneer,* many "children of the state are kept from schools because of the cost of books."[7] These were the first states to allow women to hold school offices, like that of county superintendent, and the first to give women the right to vote in school elections and in general statewide elections as well. With so much firsthand experience with undemocratic treatment, it seems only predictable that the people of the Great Plains would be pioneers in the extension of democracy.

It is significant, too, that the leaders of the Populist movement saw their undertaking as the orchestration of a mass educational effort. "Our organization is a school," maintained Charles Macune. And he meant it. His weekly *National Economist* was literally a textbook for hundreds of thousands of farmers across the country, but especially in the trans-Mississippi West. Together with their poverty and powerlessness, Macune's text provided ample points of departure for systematic inquiry into the policies directing American society. Forty thousand suballiance groups dotted the American countryside. Alliance-trained "lecturers" visited nearly all of them, providing systematic instruction to "develop the requisite intellectual tools" for "a systematic analysis of the causes of poverty and the mutual construction of cooperative solutions."[8] Macune instructed Populist lecturers to lead farmers in lessons about the political and economic circumstances that impinged on their lives. Michael N. Johnson provides an example of one lesson engaged in by countless farmers across the country:

Using data from the 1790 through 1880 census reports Macune had the students engage in a mathematics exercise in which they first calculated the growth in population and national wealth from 1790 to 1880. Next, of course, he had them compare their own and their neighbors' per capita wealth with that they had just derived from the government's 1880 census data. The great discrepancies between the "average" wealth in the nation and their own absolute impoverishment were readily apparent to all in attendance. The lecturers were then instructed to lead a discussion around questions such as: How does this inequality occur? Why does it persist? Should so few have so much while so many have so little?[9]

Through concerted educational effort, the leaders of the Populist movement tried to orchestrate a massive extension of democracy; that is, they tried to turn the focus of government back to the interests of the people. They called for the direct election of senators, limited terms in office, a graduated income tax, and tightened controls over price gouging by railroads. They promoted group buying and selling to consolidate what little power they had in the so-called free market. They encouraged farmers to pool their resources and insure themselves and their crops, rather than supporting wealthy insurance houses, and most significantly, they created a sophisticated "subtreasury" plan that would allow farmers to bypass exploitive bankers and still obtain the credit they needed. The system called for the construction of a network of grain warehouses as well as the provision of government loans to farmers on the basis of the grain deposited in those warehouses. It might have worked.

Regrettably, the momentum of the Populist movement was co-opted by the Democratic Party and its 1896 presidential candidate, William Jennings Bryan. One other Populist demand was for the free coinage of silver in order to ease the burden of years' worth of currency contraction. Bryan and the Democrats adopted the "silver plank" and were able to convince the Populists to throw their support to Bryan. Even with this support, however, Bryan lost. The strength of the movement was therefore spent. The Populist "threat" was over.

The election of 1896 is well worth examining, for perhaps more than any other election before or since (with the possible exceptions of 1796 and 1800), it epitomized a race between commerce and agriculture. This was the first election marked by professional campaign managers, manipulated media messages, advertising, and so on. William McKinley's campaign manager, Marcus Hanna, spent millions of dollars in his successful bid for McKinley's election. This was in rather sharp contrast to Bryan's budget of $300,000. More than this, however, Hanna played off the fears of industrialists about the inflation they thought would take place when Bryan infused silver into the economy. Many large employers in urban settings threatened mass layoffs if Bryan was elected. Emotions ran deep. In the background, the country was going through a terrible depression. The Panic of 1893 had created widespread unemployment, as high as 25 percent. There were bitter and brutal workplace strikes across the country. Many corporations, even some rail companies that had vastly overextended themselves, closed their doors. Trade unionism was growing at unprecedented rates, as was the American Socialist Party. Together with the Populist threat, there was an intense sense of insecurity on the part of some, of possibility on the part of others.

The nagging sense of insecurity proved more powerful, although the election of 1896 was close. McKinley received 7,035,000 votes to Bryan's 6,467,000. The strategies that Hanna pioneered have since become common practice; that is, through enough advertising, certain ideas are raised to the status of common sense by campaign managers. In this case, anything other than the "gold standard" in monetary policy was depicted as immoral, and a vote for McKinley was seen as a vote for the maintenance of "national honor." With hindsight, of course, it is obvious that this was ridiculous, a meaningless shibboleth, but it nevertheless set in motion a new marriage between government and industry—a marriage that has been entrenched for so long now that the American people find it culturally difficult to imagine another alternative. Whereas Enlightenment liberal ideas called for a laissez-faire policy, keeping government out of the economic sphere, a new version of liberalism was ushered in with the twentieth century. This is often referred to as "corporate liberalism," for it unabashedly enlisted government support for the cause of corporate expansion.

There was another powerful circumstance, this one ideological, that seemed to call for this marriage. Since Charles Darwin's 1859 publication of *The Origin of Species*, organic rather than mechanistic metaphors were increasingly used to describe the way societies work. Americans no longer spoke of making "republican machines" of schoolchildren or of the "machinery of state." They spoke more about the survival of the fittest and about adapting to changing circumstances. To the Social Darwinists of the turn of the century, American society was an organism, not a machine, and from all the evidence available during the 1890s—urban ghettos, pollution, corruption, populism, socialism, strikes, violence, depression, and unemployment—the organism was in sad shape. The fact that these views were wrapped in the cloak of science brought that much more intensity to pervasive anxieties, particularly within the commercial-industrial class.

It is easy to see why contemporaries felt that there was so much at stake in the outcome of the 1896 election. And, indeed, a victory for Bryan might have changed the course of U.S. history significantly. But McKinley and the nation's industrial leaders persevered, and soon thereafter (1898) the country was caught up in a war of questionable origin with Spain, a weak, former superpower. The conflict spurred the economy, and soon jobs were plentiful again. In fact, immigration resumed at unprecedented rates during the first decade of the twentieth century. Although the momentum of populism was defused and the movement was then brought to a halt, many of the reforms the Populists advocated eventually came into being, albeit premised on terms most beneficial to the industrial interests of the country.

*   *   *

The extent to which popular opinion considered the American republican experiment at great risk during the 1890s should not be underestimated. The Progressive Era that followed this decade put the country on a path that led it further from the democratic ideals upon which it had been founded, as was noted in Chapter 3. As risks are heightened, democracy erodes. The uncertainty that pervaded the 1890s quite logically gave birth to the Progressive Era emphasis on experts and expert commissions. Darwinian logic seemed to legitimate the perception that some people were of a better sort than others, better suited to adapt to changing circumstances, more "fit" in an evolutionary sense. The burden of "progressing" out of the economic and social vortex created during the 1890s rested heavily on this group of emerging elites, or so they claimed. Harvard University president Charles Eliot argued that schools must "train the minds of the children that when they become adults they should . . . have respect for the attainments of experts in every branch of governmental, industrial, and social activity."[10] Demonstrating the proper deference to experts trained in the newly popular "scientific management" was ostensibly the mark of an educated person. Meritocracy, rather than democracy, was increasingly seen as the only way to manage the health of a large, complex organism like the United States.

To this end, in a society equipped with the appropriate scientific tools (among them the IQ test), social engineering was deemed possible. In fact, in the name of social engineering, both workplace and school were radically transformed, and the similarities between the two after transformation went beyond physical appearances. Just as work in the nation's factories was divided up into its lowest skill elements, school gradations became more pronounced and lockstep, and even curriculum was broken down into its lowest conceptual elements, a circumstance that evolved easily into the idea of "behavioral objectives." The decisionmaking that accompanied industrial production was removed from workers and placed in the hands of the expert managers. And since the experts' perception was that there was plenty of work available for those without much intellectual capacity, a school curricular track tailored to this sort of person was thought to be necessary. In other words, schools were to provide learning experiences that matched the "evident and probable destinies" of students, to use a common Progressive Era locution. The "common school" fell by the wayside because now, in a truly progressive era, schooling needed to be comprehensive, with its programs tailored to all levels of learners.

Handing the fate of American society over to experts required that neighborhood school boards be collapsed into citywide centralized boards of six or seven individuals. This small group of elites, in turn, hired the services of a highly trained educational expert called a school superintendent. City managers, at-large city councils, and any and all methods tending toward the centralization of decisionmaking were thought to be (1) efficient and therefore always desirable and (2) eminently wise, in that they facilitated the use of expert judgment.

The experts who took over the decisionmaking processes in the United States were often presidential appointees. Both Presidents William Taft and Theodore Roosevelt created an extraordinary number of expert commissions to solve one problem or another. One of Roosevelt's commissions was assigned the task of solving the "rural problem." It was not exactly clear what the rural problem was when the Country Life Commission began its work in 1908. In time, however, it became understood that the problem was the already identifiable trend of cityward migration of American farm youth. A famous horticulturalist at Cornell University, Liberty Hyde Bailey, was asked by Roosevelt to head the new commission. In Bailey's view, the problem to be addressed was how to develop and maintain "on our farms a civilization in full harmony with the best American ideals." Another famous Country Life advocate, Mabel Carney of Illinois, framed the issue this way: "The rural problem, in its most important aspects, is the problem of maintaining a standard people on our farms."[11] The report of the commission itself described the problem as one of preserving "a race of men in the open country that, in the future as in the past, will be the stay and strength of the nation in time of war, and its guiding and controlling spirit in time of peace."[12]

By 1900, intellectuals had already identified the farm-to-city trend among rural youth. In fact, the issue was brought to the attention of the general public by the tremendously popular literary works of Hamlin Garland. *Main Travelled Roads* (1893) was a collection of short stories that vividly portrayed the migration of rural talent down well-traveled roads to the city. *Prairie Folks* (1899) was a less than complimentary account of the drudgery of farm life that led to cityward migration.

On a more scientific level, the demise of agriculture on a percentage basis within the population sounded an alarm among social evolutionists. The publication of Wilbert Anderson's *The Country Town: A Study of Rural Evolution* (1906) clearly spoke of the dangers of the new industrial order. Said Anderson, rural communities were "vital parts of the economic organism of the world." Their health was in jeopardy, however, if, as he predicted, the "first effect" of industrialized agriculture was to be the "departure of the farmer's boy from the home." Bailey saw the situation this way: "The city sits like a parasite, running out its roots into the open country and draining it of its substance. Mankind has not yet worked out this organic relation of town and country."[13]

It is difficult to overemphasize the depths to which Darwinian thinking went on the subject of organisms and the need for scientific expertise to promote their health and growth. Schoolchildren were sometimes compared to cells—each with a certain function to play—in the societal organism. Given such a belief, the idea of a *comprehensive*, rather than *common*, school system, designed to serve those destined for unskilled labor as well as those destined for highly skilled positions, held a great deal of currency.

At the core of the Country Life movement was the idea that rural areas must not become "fished out ponds populated chiefly by bullheads and suckers," to use the expression of a prominent American sociologist.[14] Rural areas needed to remain viable and vibrant, lest the organism that was American society become ill and begin to deteriorate. Again, Bailey clearly depicted why stopping the cityward trend of rural youth was so important: "Civilization oscillates between two poles. At one extreme is the so-called laboring class, and at the other are the syndicated and corporate and monopolized interests. Between these two poles is the great agricultural class, which is the natural balance-force or the middle wheel of society."[15] "Folk depletion," as many sociologists referred to cityward migration, would inhibit the power of the agricultural class to perform this vital, stabilizing function. If one viewed society as an organism, this depletion could hasten serious societal deterioration. Something needed to be done to prevent the trend from going too far. A kind of social engineering was deemed necessary, and thus another "expert commission" (the Country Life Commission) was created, with Liberty Hyde Bailey at its head.

*　　*　　*

As with almost all attempts at social engineering, the public school was a logical starting point. During the 1980s, for example, when the government wanted to reduce illicit drug use, a program was initiated to encourage youth to "Just say no." Although considerably more sophisticated, the reform agenda of the Country Lifers nevertheless shared certain similarities with this now-famous brainchild of a former First Lady. Country Life creeds were established, and thousands of schoolchildren across the nation were asked to begin their days by pledging their belief that "the Country which God made is more beautiful than the City man made [and] that opportunity comes as often to a boy on the farm as often as to a boy in the city." The idea was to make rural kids satisfied and content with rural life.

Country Life advocates went considerably beyond the creation of pledges and slogans, however. In keeping with emerging ideas related to schooling and how people learn (for example, the "Progressive" educational philosophy of John Dewey), they began to talk about the relevance of subject matter to individual students. "New educators" claimed that what children already knew profoundly influenced what they would come to know. Lessons developed with agriculture in mind were strongly encouraged at teachers' institutes and normal schools throughout the first twenty-five years of this century.

Liberty Hyde Bailey advocated "nature studies" as a way to keep rural youth in tune with the natural rhythms that governed agricultural life. In this way, it was hoped, education might contribute to promoting a love of the countryside in rural children, an emotion deemed necessary to effectively counter the seduction of bright lights and big cities. A popular 1915 education textbook, written with future rural teachers in mind, put the matter this way:

> [T]he greatest problem before us today is the conservation of the boys and girls of the state for the rural community. It cannot afford to lose so many of its brightest young men and women. One of the best ways to keep them is to interest them in their environment by teaching them more subjects they can use and fewer that have no practical bearing on daily life.[16]

Curriculum, more than pledges, was one of two major educational thrusts of the Country Life movement.

The second push was in the area of rural school consolidation, and this has resulted in a great deal of confusion concerning the movement. Indeed, because of this emphasis, many have viewed the Country Life agenda as an attempt to urbanize rural schools.[17] If the matter is well looked into, one can see that this view holds little merit. As Mabel Carney suggested, "What we need and must have, to solve the problem of rural education, is not an urban school whose influences lead young people of the farms directly away from the land, but a country school, a country school improved, modernized, and adopted to the needs of present country life."[18]

The rural school consolidation touted by Country Lifers was geared toward the neighborhood level. Rather than supporting five or six struggling small districts in a given township, for example, Country Lifers advocated consolidation that would result in two or three small, healthy districts. With better roads and better transportation, it was deemed feasible to position schools so that families might live as far as four or maybe even five miles from the schoolhouse. Today, of course, consolidation decisions are routinely made that put students in excess of thirty miles from their school. It is fair to say that Country Lifers advocated limited rural school consolidation, but they would have been vehemently opposed to the horrendous extensions that now shadow the concept.

As with most historical developments, the Country Life movement was both good and bad. There is much to be said for tailoring curriculum in a manner that yields relevance from all that is studied. There was clearly room for limited consolidation as well. But in other ways, however, the Country Life Commission was an example of a conscious, concerted effort to move the circumstances of American life out of the hands of the people themselves and into the hands of experts. Although the commissioners purportedly listened to country people, their task was solely to solve the "rural problem." Many rural residents rejected what to them was a stinging form of condescension. A popular periodical, the *American Farm Review*, had this to say about the commission:

> Nobody goes farther than the American Farm Review in commending any plan for the improvement of rural life. Any measure having for its object the greater efficiency of country schools, the improvement of roads, the telephone and rural delivery service, the extension of libraries, and so on, meets with our unqualified approval. But we are of the opinion that farm life can be improved only through the continued material advancement of the farmers. No commission can elevate it, or even show the farmer the way. In the future, as in the past, the farmer must work out his own salvation.[19]

An editor of *Country Gentleman* added, "We don't particularly relish being told in one breath that we are the salt of the earth, that on us and our labors rest the foundations of the economic structure of the business and politics of the nation, and in the next breath that we are isolated, lonely, groping in dark ways, and need a commission of professors to inquire into our malady."[20]

This reliance on experts invaded both the school and the factory. Decisionmaking was reserved for those "at the top." Taking orders was the exclusive province of those at the bottom. Darwinian logic suggested that this was as it should be. This viewpoint still lingers powerfully today. For example, I frequently ask a classroom full of undergraduate college students why women do not constitute one-half of the U.S. Congress. Although there are always a few who answer with some intellectual sophistication, the far more predictable answer is that men are somehow "more fit" for the job. Not only do we rely heavily on Darwinian logic, we actually employ Darwinian rhetoric.

The comprehensive school system we now possess is a direct outgrowth of the evolutionary ideology that pervaded our country during the Progressive Era. Teachers were on the lowest rung of the ladder. Their task was to take orders, not to make decisions. We are only now, at the very end of the twentieth century, beginning to show signs of success in a long struggle to change this circumstance.

*   *   *

Considering that the goal of the Country Life Commission was to put a halt to the trend of cityward migration by rural youth, the movement must be considered a failure. Clearly, the "unsettling" of the countryside went on pretty much unabated throughout this century. Despite the best efforts of Country Life advocates, farmers went from representing roughly 40 percent of the population at the century's outset to constituting less than 2 percent at the century's close. In the process, the country went from supporting some 140,000 school districts to supporting just 16,000. In other words, "consolidation" has been a defining characteristic of educational history throughout the twentieth century. This characteristic was driven by a powerful assumption, albeit an unsubstantiated one, concerning the best way to go about the business of public schooling. And that assumption is that "bigger is better." Throughout the century, this unsupported educational policy was vehemently espoused even though it was demonstrably unkind to communities. We are finally reaching the point where many thoughtful people have acquired the necessary intellectual perspective to see this circumstance as a terrible tragedy—a tragedy that continues to haunt us in the form of enormous social costs.

The nation underwent profound changes during the twentieth century for a variety of reasons. The emphasis on national economies, stemming all the way back to Adam Smith, led to a worldwide scramble for colonies and natural resources. As a result of twentieth-century technological developments, the century was marred by recurring episodes of total war, by wars in which such folks as "noncombatants" no longer existed. The death and destruction that has followed in the wake of competitive national economies butting heads has been unparalleled throughout human history.

The shift to a "global economy" and the appearance of multinational corporations may have reduced the odds of an impending World War III (though this is far from certain), but these new global features have created other circumstances that forewarn of equally deep, equally catastrophic instabilities. Anxiety about environmental disaster in the pursuit of profit, for instance, is now widespread and seems to have simply become a substitute for the decades-long threat of a nuclear holocaust.

We might have heeded such economists as Jane Jacobs or E. F. Schumacher when the destruction attendant on the pursuit of national economies became obvious. They would have had us turn, not to a global economy but back to local economies, where size and scale are manageable and where the health of the environment can receive the attention it deserves. Instead, the fate of communities in the global economy is no better now than in the days when we insisted on attending to a national economy. The situation is worse, in fact. Manufacturing plants readily cross international borders in pursuit of dirt-cheap labor and lax environmental standards. There is no sign of any allegiance to community among the great multinational corporations of the world. If they can get away with it, many such corporations will readily pull the retirement benefits of employees who have worked their entire adult lives for the benefit of the corporation.

All of this is painfully clear, as are the enormous disparities between the wealthy and the poor in the United States, a development that has taken place in just the past fifteen years, a time period that marks the history of our embrace of the "global" economy. There is no need to recite the facts about real income loss for 60 percent of the population during the Reagan and Bush years and extraordinary gains for the top 20 percent.[21] There is no need to say again that the 1990s political agenda has sought to make a virtue out of taking from the poor (welfare cuts) and giving to the rich (repealing capital gains taxes). These things are widely known.

The last time the people had the power, potentially at least, to change these circumstances, however, was during the agrarian revolt that was populism. If the people are ever to regain the government that is supposed to be of, by, and for them, then that will require a different way of doing business within our educational system. If this is ever to happen, it will likely take place first in the rural environment, for a variety of reasons. Wendell Berry, thinking similarly, maintains that

> if improvement is going to begin anywhere, it will have to begin out in the country and in the country towns. This is not because of any intrinsic virtue that can be ascribed to rural people, but because of their circumstances. Rural people are living, and have lived for a long time, at the site of the trouble. They see all around them every day, the marks and scars of an exploitive national economy. They have much reason, by now, to know how little real help is to be expected from somewhere else. They still have, moreover, the remnants of local memory and local community. And in rural communities there are still farms and small businesses that can be changed according to the will and desire of individual people.[22]

First, over and above this, rural schools are small, and this circumstance may facilitate the shift to democratic principles. Second, rural schoolteachers know one another, and this will facilitate the kind of in-depth study required to understand how matters came to be as they are, as well as how they might become different. But this puts us ahead of the story. Renewing the rural school is the subject of the next section of this book. Before moving on to it, we should conclude this examination of public policy with the latest development in the history of the American countryside.

*   *   *

In 1953, historian Grant McConnell published a provocative book entitled *The Decline of Agrarian Democracy.* In this book, he openly wondered how the agrarian movement of the 1890s could reach such a level of power and popularity, only to dramatically disappear in a very short period of time. Had the American farmer's "appearance upon the political field of the 'nineties been only an apparition? What magic had been worked to exorcise him from that field?"[23] In short, McConnell's book is an attempt to answer his own question. The Populists had created a platform that hinged on democracy in all arenas: political, economic, educational, and social. And they did this at a time when, potentially, they possessed the wherewithal to marshal a numerical majority at the polls. What happened? Why was the Progressive Era marked by the ascendancy of business interests and the gradual shift away from democratic principles? Again, quoting McConnell:

> Certainly the decade of the 'nineties had had many of the qualities of a nightmare ... the farmer's grievances had been real, so too had his program. It would be untrue to say that at every point his program struck at fundamentals, yet equally it would be untrue to say that it entirely missed them. The strength of the reaction against the program and the lasting memory of the programs of the 'nineties as shown in the [business] trusts' paternal solicitude for the farmer during the two decades that followed are good evidence of the strength of the Populist threat.[24]

McConnell persuasively makes the case that the wedding of big business and government in the Progressive Era resulted in what amounted to a calculated rapprochement with the nation's largest farmers.

Corporate philanthropy joined with the U.S. Department of Agriculture (USDA) during the Progressive Era to create the concept of agricultural extension via the role of an agricultural expert known as the county "agent." The productivity of county agents was assessed through statistical reports. As McConnell demonstrates, this procedure served as a catalyst, prompting county agents to work with those who were seen as neighborhood leaders or with groups of such rural leaders. The end result of this was that much of the county agents' work was organizational, and as early as 1911 the term "bureau" was used to describe county agent–created organizations. Land grant universities joined the effort to be of service to successful farmers, and the universities' extension leaders gradually became the directors of all the county agents within a state. By 1920, countless county and state farm bureaus had formed a national organization called the American Farm Bureau Federation. With the establishment of a powerful organization of large and successful farmers, the rapprochement sought by the elite decisionmakers of the Progressive Era was achieved:

> Although the Populist threat had disappeared, the memory of it was still vivid to the grain exchanges, heads of farm equipment trusts, and directors of banks. It is even likely that some of these outfits glimpsed the possibility of enlisting organized agriculture, or rather, reorganized agriculture on the side of capitalism. Whether or not there was such a deliberate intention, few better means to accomplish the result could be imagined than the course that was followed.[25]

The combination of corporate industries, the U.S. government, and land grant universities enabled the creation of a farmer organization that was concerned almost exclusively with profit and that bought in, wholesale, to the predominant thinking about the utilization of expertise. The concern for social justice in the name of democracy was gone. More than any other factor, I believe, this circumstance condemned family farming to the gradual, and now nearly complete, takeover by corporate farming interests. Marty Strange made a similar point when he argued that there was a time when "the cause of common people and the cause of farmers was synonymous." Since that time farmers have played no role in the significant social movements of this century.[26]

There have been other factors besides the abandonment of democratic principles behind the deterioration of life in the countryside, and they deserve mention. The first is World War I. From its beginning in 1914, the war was an enormous blow to European and Russian agriculture. For the United States, which did not become involved in the war until late 1917, it was an enormous boost. As far as extending the neglect of democracy and the legitimacy of expertise via the extension concept went, the war's timing could not have been better. Everywhere, farmers were looking to increase their productivity. By the war's end, the price of wheat had risen to $3.50 per bushel, a near all-time high. Farmers invested in more land, in traction engines (tractors), and in other machinery innovations. To do this, of course, they went heavily into debt. When European soldiers returned to their fields, circumstances for American farmers changed almost overnight. The price of all agricultural commodities dropped precipitously after 1920. By 1921, for example, the price of wheat had fallen to just a tad over $1 per bushel. For many American farmers, one-dollar wheat did not cover expenses. Mass foreclosures were the result. Two million Americans, or a little over 6 percent of the farm population, left the farm between 1916 and 1929.

During another era, such a demographic shift away from agriculture might well have been catastrophic. But the 1920s were quite unprecedented. It was a giddy time for most Americans. We emerged from the Great War as the world's leading creditor. Cash flow was at an all-time high, even higher than during the war years. Construction was intense; jobs were created at a tremendous clip. These circumstances helped to bury what lingering concerns there were among the general public about the serious exodus taking place across the American countryside. Neither Warren Harding nor Calvin Coolidge called for a Country Life Commission to halt the cityward migration. The dispossessed, after all, could find plenty of nonfarm work in the growing urban centers. Food was cheap, and America's diet was improving greatly, as was indicated by Coolidge's campaign slogan, "a chicken in every pot." If the soldiers couldn't be kept down on the farm after seeing "Paree," so much the better. They were better off in the city anyway, and for those who wanted to farm but couldn't, well, the American public simply wasn't interested.

Of course, the giddy expansion came to a calamitous end in 1929. The paper wealth that had buoyed expansion simply disappeared overnight. There were mass layoffs all across the country. Breadlines became a predictable feature in urban settings. Many people starved to death. The farmers who had struggled through the 1920s on the thinnest of profit margins found that prices were capable of plummeting to lows beyond their worst nightmares. By 1932, commodity prices for farmers were roughly one-half their 1929 level.

Although this seems counterintuitive, the farm population actually grew during the depression. The statistics are deceptive, however, for farmers lost their farms at a rapid rate, but where were they to go? There were no jobs in the cities. All too often, once-proud farm owners became tenants of the insurance companies or the banking houses that ended up with the defaulted farm mortgages. The Joads of Steinbeck's *The Grapes of Wrath* represent a fair example of a common trend. Indeed, by 1935, one-half of Iowa's farmers were tenants.[27]

With the price of wheat at 40 cents per bushel and corn down to 20 cents, it is not surprising that many residents of the Great Plains states migrated to the West Coast. Multiple years of drought encouraged the exodus. Unlike its response in the 1920s, this time the American public was very concerned with what was happening in the countryside. People were hungry. Food, and thus farms, was very much on their minds. Agricultural policy became a pivotal political issue during the depression, and to some extent, it has remained so ever since.

President Franklin D. Roosevelt instituted a variety of reforms, including price supports, to alleviate the worst of the depression tendencies. Although circumstances for farmers improved slightly during the middle of the 1930s, circumstances were once again quite severe by the decade's end. Even with the nation's first acreage reduction program, commodity surpluses lingered (in part because citizens at home and abroad had no money to buy the food they needed), holding prices down. The decade closed with circumstances not much better than they had been in 1932. On the bright side, if one is callous enough to look at it in this way (and, regrettably, some Americans were—"It's good for the economy" became a popular expression), war broke out in Europe. The United States was well poised to become the "world's breadbasket" once again. It was a role we would play on the national scene until the 1980s.

The 1950s were like the 1920s in many respects. The nonfarm economy boomed, and the American public became, yet again, fairly oblivious to agricultural questions. Farmers avoided a severe postwar depression with the price supports first begun during the New Deal. But these supports, as they had during the 1930s, brought about very troublesome surpluses. And as before, the government began to pay farmers to take acres out of production. Farmers worked through the 1950s and the first years of the 1960s as they had during the 1920s, on the thinnest of profit margins. Year after year with these meager profits culminated in a mass exodus, once again, from the nation's farms. Farmers left the countryside at a record pace during the 1960s, and because the nation was embroiled in serious domestic and foreign disputes, the American public took little notice.

Rapid technological advances during this decade meant that the remaining farmers were able to pick up the slack caused by the loss of millions of farmers. Farm size began to increase dramatically, and circumstances that arose during the next decade, the 1970s, would add even more fuel to this trend. In 1972, to everyone's great surprise, the surpluses that had plagued American agriculture since the end of World War II were suddenly gone. Foreign customers, most notably the Soviet Union, were lining up ready to pay cash for agricultural commodities. Prices skyrocketed. Soybeans, for example, climbed to nearly $13 per bushel. There was no doubt about the fact that a boom had arrived. The secretary of agriculture boldly announced that farmers ought to plow from "fencerow to fencerow" and that small farmers should either "get big or get out." Although there were many older farmers around the country who knew, firsthand, that busts follow booms, this wasn't the prediction one was likely to hear from the USDA or any lending agency. Land prices rose dramatically, and farmers borrowed heavily, based on the paper equity of rising land values.

The eminently predictable had arrived by 1981, aided as it was by our quandary over the Soviet invasion of Afghanistan and the resulting grain embargoes a few years earlier. Farmers went out of business at a rate that approached the figures for the 1960s. Iowa, for example, lost 20 percent of its farmers during the 1980s. In fact, since the 1930s, when "agricultural policy" became a permanent fixture in American politics, the number of farmers in the United States has steadily declined. This circumstance ought to lead us to ask, "Are we so poor at creating policy?" Or at the very least, we might ask, "Do we not have the wherewithal to learn from our mistakes or must we repeat them decade after decade?"

Although these seem like the obvious questions, there are a few other variables to consider before addressing them. First, whereas farmer profits declined to the point where millions could no longer afford to continue farming, Americans have enjoyed the lowest food prices of any country in the industrialized world. Second, whereas farmers have gone out of business, agribusinesses have made such enormous profits and have expanded so rigorously that several are now among the world's largest multinational corporations. For the people of the countryside, by and large, American farm policy has been a huge failure. Along with the disappearance of American farmers came closed schools, hospitals, clinics, newspapers, hardware stores, and lumberyards—and the list could go on and on. The flip side to this story, of course, is that to America's commercial interests, farm policy has been a tremendous boon. The corporate appetite has been insatiable for decades, and it remains so. For instance, minimizing farmer profits in order to maximize corporate gains is no longer enough. Through the use of what economists have termed, innocuously enough, "vertical integration," agribusinesses are now actively seeking to replace farmers. That is, they are trying to create huge farms to generate their own supply of commodities to process and then, in turn, want to create their own grocery stores to sell their products. Writing in 1990, Osha Gray Davidson described one such corporate integration attempt:

> ConAgra is the nation's leading distributor of pesticides. It is also the country's number one flour miller and number one producer and marketer of frozen prepared foods, and in 1988 it became the nation's top beef slaughterer. Because companies like ConAgra are in the fortunate position of selling inputs to farmers and buying outputs from them wholesale, they are able to benefit doubly from policies that encourage all-out production. As farmers were going bankrupt in the early 1980s, ConAgra reported record sales and earnings each year.[28]

Of course, this circumstance is merely a predictable feature of the trend chronicled in Chapters 4–6. No student attending a rural school should graduate without a close inspection of developments such as this.

*   *   *

The very idea of the nation's food supply being concentrated in the hands of a few "for-profit" corporations makes a sham of the notion of freedom. This is not immediately obvious because we have been socialized into a shallow conception of freedom as "freedom from." If we had listened to Gerrard Winstanley and the many agrarian thinkers who have followed his lead, we might have concerned ourselves more with "freedom to"—the freedom to live one's life productively and comfortably in the community of one's familial heritage, for instance. This could and should have been a policy goal in this country. If it had been, we wouldn't be looking at building prisons today as a kind of "economic development."

The dire societal and environmental circumstances we currently face are tied to our cultural embrace of Lockean possessive individualism. This emphasis put the interest of the individual above the interests of the community. Because community is so pivotal to the development of character, morality, and virtue, and because our policies have been so destructive of it, we are now left with a citizenry little practiced at shouldering responsibility and thereby unused to marshaling the qualities that add up to substantive character.

This look at public policy and the subordination of community was intended to show that deliberate choices have been made over the past cou-

ple of centuries and that these choices have almost always resulted in enhanced power and profit accruing in the urban commercial sector.
Alternatives to these choices have always been there, whether it was when
Oliver Cromwell looked at the options delineated by Hobbes and
Winstanley, when emerging American elites examined the options presented
by Alexander Hamilton and Thomas Jefferson, or when their descendants
compared the programs offered by our first generation of societal engineers
with the Populists' agenda. In each case, the choices made have been those
that rejected democratic principles in favor of such things as Darwinian
logic or an imaginary cultural conception called "progress."

If we are to avoid further social and environmental deterioration in this
society, we need to execute a grassroots-level cultural shift away from a
conception of freedom as "freedom from" to a conception of "freedom to."
First and foremost on that list would be the freedom to have a voice in the
decisions that affect one's community and thereby one's life. In other words,
democracy must be a standard by which we begin to guide and measure our
lives, rather than using material accumulation for that purpose. "Virtuous"
must become our highest accolade rather than "successful." The notion of
successfulness presupposes the unsuccessful, and this partially explains why
a larger percentage of our population is behind bars than in any other nation in the world.

In order to begin to execute this cultural shift back to a community orientation guided by democratic principles, several things must be acknowl-
edged. The first is that it will take years to accomplish. The second is that
the current seats of power will not likely be disposed to be of much help.
The third is that the very idea is so countercultural that it will take a good
deal of concerted study just to be able to understand the problem, let alone
get on to the business of democratically deliberating solutions.

All of these caveats suggest that the rural school is the place to begin the
process. Schools offer twelve years of enculturation for the nation's youth.
In the past, this enculturation has tended toward legitimating the pursuit of
"success." Twelve years of enculturation into an ethic of shouldering mutual obligations in the interest of the health and well-being of a place, while
nurturing an allegiance to the community, can go a long way toward creating the kind of cultural shift we are talking about. The second caveat—that
there won't be much help available—is simply business as usual for rural
schools. They have never received much help—just the opposite, in fact.
The third caveat—that the goal requires widespread intellectual wherewithal (the original educational ideal in liberal theory)—also suggests the
school as the agent of change. Rural teachers are, or ought to be, the stew-
ards of the intellectual life in their communities. To use current terminol-
ogy, rural communities must become "learning organizations," and rural
teachers are the obvious candidates for helping make this happen.

Of course, there will be those who say that the task is too large or that the kind of intellectual wherewithal described in this book is simply beyond the ability of the average rural citizen to grasp. Although the task is indeed large and although we have allowed ourselves to become unfamiliar with discourse related to ethics and justice, history unequivocally rejects the assumption that the task cannot be accomplished. The aggrieved farmers of the plains demonstrated a powerful allegiance to democracy a century ago. Sociologist Seymour Martin Lipset has demonstrated that during the post–World War II era, the rural dwellers on the plains of Canada, especially in Saskatchewan, went through their own successful experiment with cooperatives, their own period of heightened social consciousness and allegiance to democracy, only to be thwarted, as were the American Populists, by the growing power of corporations and banks. According to Lipset, Saskatchewan

> farmers are interested in their society and its relation to the rest of the world. Winter after winter, when the wheat crop is in, thousands of meetings are held throughout the province by political parties, churches, farmers' educational associations, and cooperatives. There are informal gatherings, also, in which farmers discuss economic and political problems. Not hedged in by the necessity of punching a time clock daily, these farmers, who have come from every part of Europe and North America, have frequent sessions in which they consider the ideas of Adam Smith, Karl Marx, William Morris, Henry George, James Kiel Hardie, William Jennings Bryan, Thorstein Veblen, and others. Almost every English-speaking farmer subscribes to three or four farm weeklies, which are veritable storehouses of economic and political debate. In their correspondence columns the more literate and vociferous farmers argue the merits of religion, systems of government, the Soviet Union, socialism, socialized medicine, Social Credit, and schemes for marketing wheat. In traveling about the province I soon learned not to be surprised when a farmer whom I was interviewing would open a book by Morris, Henry George, Veblen, Major C. H. Douglas or some other technical social scientist.[29]

The argument that average people can't muster the requisite intellectual power is clearly ahistorical nonsense, but this doesn't change the fact that mobilizing that power will be a tall order. Part Three of this book speaks directly to the role the rural school might play in mobilizing that power.

Part Three

Education and the Renewal of Community

7

Starting the Conversation

Let us answer this book of ink with a book of flesh and blood.
—Ralph Waldo Emerson, 1841

At last the point has been reached where the rural school can be factored into the larger themes of the book. In Part One, three elements that served to build and sustain rural communities over centuries were worked through. In Part Two, the policy trends that undermined these elements and thereby destroyed or severely diminished rural communities were explored. This third part of the book deals specifically with the work of rebuilding these communities upon an educational rather than an economic foundation. This should not be simplistically misconstrued, however, as a call to ignore economic concerns. Rather, it is a call to recognize that history tells us, fairly unequivocally, that economic justice rests on widely distributed intellectual and deliberative power. Educational theory, therefore, ought not to trail behind prevailing economic wisdom; it should be the other way around. This idea is essentially the rejected educational agenda of Winstanley, Jefferson, and other agrarian spokespersons. If we continue to reject their arguments supporting education as a catalyst in the development of civic virtue, there is little reason to hope that we might alter the trend away from democracy in contemporary politics and economics. If the people cannot speak or if they will not be heard when they do so, the overt exploitation of rural places will continue unabated.

The industrially focused school that grew out of the Progressive Era legitimated inattention to the immediate locality. Given what we know today about how people learn, we can see this development as pedagogically unsound, for it minimizes the role of background knowledge, cultural messages, and all of that which could be used to connect to the day-to-day lives of youth. But if the goal is to outfit children for successful careers in an industrial political economy, then inattention to place becomes both understandable and predictable. It contributes to our excessively mobile society, wherein career must come before family and where the propensity for unconditional commitment is almost impossible to witness.

There is an undue focus on the self in our society, and the predictable result is disintegrating neighborhoods and a vanishing sense of community. The rural and inner-city places that have suffered the most can no longer afford to be among the purveyors of this brand of individualism. Concepts like commitment, allegiance, and obligation must reenter conversations concerning the fate of these places. All communities have needs, and we must begin to enculturate youth into an ethic of shouldering responsibility for meeting these needs. This can be a large part of the educational agenda all across the country, but it has the best chance of catching on in rural America, where size is still manageable and where lingering vestiges of a sense of community yet remain.

But it will not be easy. For one thing, schooling that is geared toward producing leverage in the economic market has many decades' worth of institutional momentum. This will not be changed by merely wishing it to happen. Additionally—and this is very important—schools are not the only ideational institution in this society. The print and broadcast media will continue to send cultural messages intended to maximize their own profits. As Joshua Meyrowitz has persuasively argued, the media, therefore, represent a huge contribution to placelessness in American society.[1] Placelessness erodes our ability to commit to much of anything other than our own self-interest, and as a result, we have become a society marked by few allegiances and almost no propensity to shoulder mutual obligations. The only answer to the quandary posed by the socializing power of the media is the long-term enculturation potential of the school. That is, if the next generation is prepared in schools to understand community as a responsibility and as a commitment rather than as a hindrance or an obstacle, its members may well demand more than the cultural decadence that currently pervades print and broadcast media in this country.

But how? How does the status quo get changed? Fortunately, we are at the point in this business when we have the good sense to ask this question. Not so many years ago, educational researchers simply took new ideas out to the schools, assuming that everyone there would gratefully run with the proposed changes. Armies of would-be reformers assumed that the persuasiveness of their theoretical arguments would win people over in short order and that the end result would be educational reform. Today we can at last see these efforts as extraordinarily naive.

Many renowned scholars, including John Goodlad, Theodore Sizer, Seymour Sarason, and Michael Fullan, have distinguished themselves by providing powerful insights into the question of how we start and how we can sustain the school change process. I rely heavily on their work for the remainder of this chapter.

*   *   *

The first step in effecting change is the introduction of new ideas. At least partially, this book was written with the hope that it would be used as a catalyst for shared study and, thereafter, shared ideas. It was with this in mind that I chose Emerson's words as an epigraph to this chapter. The project may well look like rural educational reform, but it is much, much more than that. It is a kind of societal direction-setting that people may prefer to avoid but must undertake nevertheless. A commitment to justice, a commitment to the quality and character of the next generation—these things cannot be shirked by anyone who would like to see a safe world. The very act of making good on these commitments is a step in the direction of the restoration of the shared projects that constitute community.

It should be evident that this is no trifling concern. This is not sentimental nostalgia for the "good old days." Rather, it is a practical course of action for an age when resources have become seriously depleted or polluted, when hate has reemerged as an acceptable political position, and when the profit motive has proven itself capable of superseding all other pressing human and spiritual concerns. All of this confirms that the revitalization of rural communities through curricular and pedagogical work in schools is, at bottom, a moral endeavor. It is work undertaken with the express purpose of *enhancing the quality and feel of the relationships between people.* This is not a call to love thy neighbors, though certainly ignoring this Christian dictate (through our steadfast fetish with possessive individualism) has contributed significantly to the diminution of communities. It is a call, rather, to acknowledge that community means recognition of intradependence (or interdependence within a shared place). That is, a community is a place where people who may not like one another nevertheless work together to advance the welfare of that which they hold in common.[2]

Recognizing the moral dimension of educational work is a vitally important first step. When schooling is reduced to the provision of human resources for the economic market, the moral dimension of education is reduced in significance, if not eliminated altogether. Our cultural deification of the successful extends so far as to make heroes out of wealthy individuals, despite the fact, and in some cases because of the fact, that they broke laws or ruined lives on their climb to the top. One of America's great twentieth-century intellectuals, Isaac Asimov, died at nearly the same time as one of America's wealthiest individuals, Sam Walton of Wal-Mart fame. No one will have to strain trying to recall which of the two funerals captured the newspaper headlines across the country on that day a few years ago. The answer is obvious. Although this anecdote exposes a significant cultural shortcoming in this country, what is not so obvious is how the educational system has worked to perpetuate this shortcoming. I think an interchange on a popular TV sitcom nicely captures the moral poverty of the current educational agenda. When asked by his potential father-in-law about his post-high-school plans, a young man replies: "I've got it all figured out. Four years, B.A. Five years, M.B.A. Six years, BMW."

For a variety of reasons, many of which are directly related to the history discussed in Part Two of this book, people in this country, including the teachers in our schools, have been socialized away from approaching the business of schooling as a moral endeavor. This needs to be overcome, however, lest educational change be introduced merely for the sake of some shibboleth like "higher test scores." We have been down that road many times, certainly often enough to know that it inevitably leads back to where it started. The first step, then, is to introduce new ideas and to closely follow this with a demonstration of the moral imperative that undergirds them. Wrestling with the intellectual foundation is not enough.

Anyone who is really interested in the revitalization of rural communities and is interested in using the school as a vehicle to this end will need to provide space and time for interested folks to come together to talk through this idea and, eventually, to talk it through *as a moral endeavor*. These conversations need to be as inclusive as possible; that is, they need to include both community members (people not employed at the school) and school personnel. "Planning grants" are an increasingly popular mechanism with philanthropic organizations today. The reason for this is that such organizations recognize that in order to be successful with whatever work the real grant will require, conversations related to it need to be extended as far as possible.

There is really no way to rush the conversation stage. It can be made more productive, however, by assigning certain themes to meetings, with each meeting ideally preceded by shared readings related to it. As an example, a first meeting might be called to explore the topic of community revitalization through the school, and any number of journal-length articles related to this topic could accompany this invitation. A second meeting might be required for further discussion of the initial topic or perhaps the group might be ready after one meeting to move on to discuss the moral foundation of the topic. John Goodlad's 1991 Kohlberg Memorial Lecture entitled "The Moral Dimensions of Schooling and Teacher Education"[3] might make a good shared reading for this discussion.

Probably the biggest obstacle to be overcome in the initial conversations is the almost irrational desire for the quick fix. Rural communities declined as a result of many years' worth of policy decisions made with no thought for the particularity of rural places. The restoration of rural communities will come about only when policy decisions that celebrate community, in recognition of its pivotal role in the maintenance of democracy, begin to accumulate. This won't happen on a consistent basis until the process of enculturating youth into the habit and practice of responding to community needs has been sustained for a number of years. When the burden of governing falls to the next generation, that cohort will be much better equipped to shape policy in the interest of promoting community. In the initial conversations, then, it must be made clear that people cannot make a sense of community happen overnight. This will take years, and in some significant ways, we must recognize that the full benefit of our efforts is our legacy to those who will follow us. There is some consolation, however, in the words of Reinhold Niebuhr: "Anything worth doing will not be accomplished in a lifetime."[4]

Still, significant and positive fallout can happen fairly quickly. A few teachers dedicated to their school and to their community can make a difference in a hurry, especially if they receive the encouragement and support of community members and school administrators. Chapters 8 and 9 in this book are devoted to concrete ideas that dedicated teachers might try.

If the possibility of setting up an inclusive forum for in-depth conversations simply does not exist, teachers can begin to lead by example. There are stories of this happening all across the country. In many such cases, administrators and community members find themselves in the position of having to hop on board so as not to be left behind. A proactive agenda on the part of administrators can have positive results as well. Again, there are countless examples of charismatic leaders who have "turned around" poor schools. It has been my experience, however, that the best chances for success are found on the long road, the one marked by drawn-out discussions, lengthy meetings, controversy, conflict, and ultimately, solutions. It is helpful if, at some point along the way, participants begin to see that the means to sustain the commitment to community, the very thing that they are struggling to muster, is precisely the same thing they are seeking to develop and nurture in the next generation.

Discussion related to the moral dimensions undergirding the agenda of rural community revitalization through schooling can easily be used as a springboard to some of the intellectual foundations discussed in the first two sections of this book. Exploring such topics as the notion of intradependence, the negative psychological and cultural consequences of converting time into a commodity, or the ramifications of glorifying risk taking is not easy, and it would be unwise to broach these subjects at the very first meeting devoted to the revitalization agenda. Regrettably, there is an ahistorical, aphilosophical anti-intellectualism that pervades our culture.[5] "The business of America is business," or so we have convinced ourselves, and people think that what the nation needs educationally, therefore, is merely that which facilitates more business. This is the sort of logic that produces such shallow national goals as "being first in the world in math and science." No one is immune from the seductive appeal of such simplicity. But for those who would like to be a part of making a difference educationally, mouthing slogans will not replace the requisite intellectual burden of study and deliberation.

This is so because truly productive education is of necessity a community endeavor, and as a society, we have lost track of what a community is. We know it is not a TV image. We know it is not as portrayed in *Leave It to Beaver*. But just what is it? Any discussion related to community will of necessity work its way back to the matter of definition. And community is one of those terms that defies easy definition. Coming to consensus on a definition requires study and discussion. The material in this book may be of some help in this regard, and there are plenty of other sources to which interested people might turn. Unlike other books, however, this one offers— and I obviously think that this is vitally important—to help the reader come to understand how the components of practically any thoughtful definition of community have eroded under a steady stream of policy designed to facilitate the pursuit of self-interest. There is a history that renders the disintegration of community understandable, even predictable. If this history is not engaged, if it is not a topic for discussion, the group will remain very much at the mercy of the following powerful, albeit intellectually vacuous, cultural message: The decline of rural communities is inevitable either because of some natural economic law or because it is simply the price of "progress."

*   *   *

Obviously, every school and every community will approach the revitalization agenda in different ways, from different angles. But once the topic is introduced, the moral foundation undergirding it represents a highly desirable (from my experience and perspective) second topic. Further discussions may revolve around issues of definition or other foundational concerns. At some point, and this will most likely occur sooner rather than later, there will be a powerful, almost irresistible, plea to get on to what it all means. The longer such a motion can be held off and the more time the group can devote to the foundational issues, the better the chances are for later success.

Thanks to the efforts of John Goodlad, Theodore Sizer, and others, there are talented individuals across the country who have studied the complexities of the school change process and are available to groups who would like an outside voice to help them work through the revitalization agenda. If the resources are there, providing such a person can be very beneficial. Generally, an outsider will be given just enough authority to occasionally redirect the group when it encounters potentially debilitating conversational trajectories. These facilitators know how to handle the predictable arguments of naysayers, the we-tried-that-and-it-doesn't-work types. Of course, outside facilitators will have to spend some time working through the particularities of rural renewal before they can be of significant help to rural districts interested in community revitalization through the school. But this should not be a difficult obstacle for these individuals to overcome.

There is a danger in describing the conversation process, and that is that it can be made to seem easy. In reality, it is far from that. Undertaking a revitalization conversation without at least a few key, deeply committed individuals would not be wise. The difficulties involved in orchestrating such an obviously countercultural conversation will quickly take their toll on those who thought they would merely invest the time required to find out what the conversation was all about. In order to keep such folks involved, there is a certain amount of push required, despite the fact that the ideas may seem very compelling. An outsider cannot provide that push. It has to come from somewhere within, from either community members, teachers, or administrators. Needless to say, the push must be tactfully administered.

Personalities will come into play in all locales. Again, there is a great deal of literature related to predictable types of personalities—the blockers, the naysayers, and so on—and it is helpful to be forewarned that such individuals tend to surface during group work. But every situation brings different circumstances, and the only thing that can be said safely regarding the conversation process is that it will not be easy. Deep commitment will be required to sustain it.

* * *

At some point, the discussion must turn to what is to be done differently in the local school. Although the options are endless, the least little change can create high levels of anxiety, enough to produce a kind of paralysis within the group. For this reason, many believe that a few ground rules should be set in advance of the discussion that outline what kinds of changes will be made in the local school. For instance, many claim that such a group should agree that "nothing is sacred" or that "anything goes," in a kind of initial brainstorming session. This is a particularly good approach for avoiding the "tinkering syndrome"—attempts to change the appearances of the status quo without changing its substance. Bold, radically different ideas free up the imagination. Such ideas should be encouraged.

There is a full range of educational innovations currently under way in various locales across the country: integrated and interdisciplinary curricula, multi-age classrooms, blocked schedules, alternative assessments, heterogeneous grouping (gifted through disabled), and so forth; all such developments could be of huge benefit to the school choosing to attend to the needs of the immediate community. To try to do all these things at once, however, would be extremely difficult.

Changing the school focus, the school culture, and, in the process, the cultural messages that emanate from schooling experiences in rural locales are things that will take years. A school may start with very minor changes. A high-school English teacher pairs up with a social studies teacher. The two decide to use a couple of novels produced by local authors to enhance the study of American history and literature. After pleading with the principal, they get back-to-back sections so that their class periods can overlap. A few elementary teachers get together to work on special community-oriented week-long lessons that are interspersed throughout the school year. During succeeding years, a few more teachers get involved with similar projects. A group of elementary teachers decides to make a presentation at the state teachers' conference. One or two secondary teachers sign up for a summer workshop presented by REAL (Rural Entrepreneurship Through Action Learning), Inc. Student-run businesses appear. Gradually, the school develops a reputation, and potential new teachers arrive for their interviews well prepared to discuss the notion of community as a curricular lens. Creativity, activity, and intellectual vitality work their way into the very "feel" of the school. Parents notice it, like it, and begin to increase their involvement in all aspects of the school.

In another scenario, a few community members find themselves every bit as smitten by the idea of community revitalization through the school as any of the teachers. The topic becomes an agenda item for a loose association of community business owners. Together with the principal and the high-school business teacher, the group plans a research project that will be engaging for the students and beneficial for the local business community at the same time. A "cash flow" study is produced. The local paper publishes the results and asks, "What can be done to keep our money at home?" The project is such a success that the group looks to the school to solve the community's day-care shortage problem. When the next school year begins, a student-run day-care service is in place, and a senior-high psychology teacher regularly transforms the operation into a laboratory for the study of human development. Because the community requires additional housing, the vocational education teacher regularly supervises the student construction of one house each school year. At the local park, a large mural depicting the history of the community has been added by an art class. Elementary students regularly clean up vacant lots in town and orchestrate a periodic recycling service as well as a systematic fire alarm testing service for the community.

These are obviously success stories, but there is nothing here that is really out of the reach of any rural school. It is not business as usual, however, and that will be enough to generate some concern and even, perhaps, some anxiety. Community residents must be reminded again and again that it is *pedagogically wise* for students to be out in the community during school hours. This is why it is impossible to overstress the need to communicate as widely as possible. Those seeking to orchestrate changes in the school must nearly knock themselves out inviting all community stakeholders, early and often, to join in the conversation.

A failing scenario is easy to create. The revitalization conversation begins largely in the school and never becomes a forum that includes a wide spectrum of community residents. A day-care business is discussed, and curricular work related to it is undertaken. Advertisements announcing the day-care service go out before school begins, and two angry parents who operate day-care businesses rush to the superintendent insisting that the school's day-care facility will have an adverse effect on their income potential. The project is immediately dropped. The teachers, who, from their own perspective, "invested" time during the summer to do the related curriculum work, are angry and demoralized. The regular community revitalization meetings, which had been primarily school meetings from the start, are now a place to vent frustration. There is idle gossip suggesting that the superintendent doesn't really want any changes, that he would like things to stay just as they are until he retires in a few years. "He certainly didn't support us," claim the disgruntled teachers. Because the meetings become marked by mean-spiritedness, attendance drops off and the meetings themselves are frequently canceled for trivial reasons. By the start of the next school year, the revitalization campaign is a distant memory.

As pessimistic as this scenario sounds, it is the most predictable of the three. Teachers who are very active in school change put a great deal of energy into their work. This is sometimes enough to generate antipathy or envy from their less-engaged peers, who, in response, will sometimes work quite tirelessly to undermine the change process. Then, too, there are always individuals who will dispute any point raised by a particular person because of a grudge carried for years. The conversations can easily become a forum for airing petty squabbles or for individuals who "like to hear themselves talk." When these things happen, the conversation becomes dominated by three or four individuals, at which point less outspoken people stop coming to the meetings. Momentum wanes. The two or three devoted people who generated the initial interest find themselves, many times, nearly convinced that the initiative has no future. No one seems to care. Everyone wants to argue or find fault with whatever is proposed. The loneliness seems overwhelming, and the temptation to give up and pack it in presses nearer. Gradually, everyone becomes vulnerable to the prevailing cultural message: All of these little places are bound to die out anyway.

This is why the moral dimension is so crucial and is something that should be engaged early on. Unless the commitment to the revitalization agenda cuts to the level of a moral imperative in everyone's life, the wherewithal for sustaining the change movement will all too quickly exhaust itself. But if people can articulate a sense of what a community is and can then come to grips with how that sense of community was eroded in the interest of commercial profit (and to the detriment of rural people), then the basis for undertaking the revitalization agenda on a moral foundation is in place.

*   *   *

So far, nothing has been said about the group coming together to create a vision or mission statement. Michael Fullan and others argue that this is something that should come later, and I believe that this is especially true in the context of rural renewal. There is much work involved in merely coming to understand the agenda of simultaneously renewing rural schools and communities. Once the agenda is widely understood, a few initial steps need to be charted in an effort to inch toward the agenda. As this process unfolds, it will be much easier to create a vision/mission statement that captures the renewal trajectory within a given place.

There are other reasons to avoid vision setting at the start. First, doing so early on can quickly polarize a group. Because such an activity is often seen as crucially important, all the interpersonal baggage within a school and community can quickly come to the fore. These matters will eventually require some manner of resolution, but there seems to be little sense in structuring in extraneous difficulties right from the start. Second, beginning work on the agenda with the creation of a vision/mission statement will set up parameters, albeit unintentionally, that may serve to constrain free thinking about the possibilities for change. As Fullan puts it, "Change is a journey, not a blueprint."[6] The word "blueprint" suggests that there is only one way to get to the destination, whereas the word "journey" suggests just the opposite, that there are many ways. In time, those who elect to make the journey will begin to see how they can reach their destination. At that point, creating the vision/mission statement makes good sense.

Some readers may be thinking that there's nothing new here—three- or four-period days, interdisciplinary curriculum, multi-age classrooms, alternative assessments, student-run businesses, heterogeneous grouping, inclusion of the "gifted" and "disabled," and so forth; these ideas have all been around for some time. My answer is both yes and no. Certainly these ideas have been around for some time, but there are reasons to believe that these reforms will be of much more consequence in the near future than they have been in the past. I'll get to these reasons in a moment. One should recognize, first, however, that these reforms are not *ends in themselves*, but rather they are the means to an end. The goal is to reculture, not merely to restructure. An attempt to restructure for the sake of restructuring will predictably end in failure. Deep-level changes require the strength that resides in moral commitment. It is hard to generate this type of commitment for the sake of a three-period school day. However, working systematically at counteracting the destructive cultural messages that suggest that urban is better than rural, that big is better than small, that more is better than less, and so forth is an idea that, in contrast, is relatively easy to build moral commitment around. But let me return to the issue of why the democratic reforms discussed above have a better chance of unseating the status quo today than they had in the past.

First, and perhaps most significantly, these reforms are currently being undertaken simultaneously with the reform of teacher education. At earlier points in our history, reforms were directed at schools, but teachers were not trained for the new system. Thus, it was a system designed to shoot itself in the foot. This problem, thanks to John Goodlad, the Holmes Group, and others, is being addressed now.

Second, we have finally come to a point in this society where short, "right answer" tests are widely coming to be seen as damaging rather than helpful, as far as education is concerned. Of course, there is a huge testing industry that does not wish to become obsolete, and this industry, coupled with an army of test-oriented university researchers, will undoubtedly twist, turn, and squirm in its attempts to recapture a kind of hegemony in educational policy that was never wise or warranted.

Third, we have simply run out of time. We have perhaps a few more decades' worth of environmental exploitation before our consumer-oriented lifestyle will have to change. The educational system created to resonate with a culture of narcissism will have to change right along with the environmental imperatives we must begin to face. Fortunately, the number of folks willing to get started working on what this education will look like increases every year.

Last, it is becoming widely understood that education is fundamentally a human endeavor. Teachers have to know their students, and further, they have to care about their students. As more and more people begin to realize this, the idea of "efficient education" or education wedded to "industrial principles" becomes more and more unthinkable.

This last point raises the question of technology in education, and thus far I have had little to say on this issue. Certainly, technology can enhance the amount of information that students might be exposed to, but a dearth of information has never been a problem that has troubled public schools. Technology can be of real help in the extent to which it can facilitate inquiry on the part of students and teachers. But if technology is viewed in terms of applying cost-benefit analysis of the type efficiency experts like to employ, then it is a poor investment for schools. Understandings are reached more "efficiently" when learners have the chance to articulate their views in the company of other learners. Technology offers little in this regard.

Twelfth-century peasants understood better than we that technology is a mixed blessing. As noted in Chapter 2, Johann Gutenberg thought his printing press would advance the glory and grandeur of the Catholic Church. Instead, some claim, it sparked the Protestant Reformation. So it is with our current fetish for telecommunication technology. It could spell the end of democratic forms of politics and social life, as fewer and fewer people come to control the information that traverses the airwaves. Or it could be a tremendous boost to democracy by eliminating the need for elected representatives, since all Americans, if they owned computers, could propose and then vote directly on legislation.

Used as a tool for research inside classrooms, technology holds great promise. But if used as a "delivery" system, technology spells educational disaster. If Americans reject the slowly developing axiom that in order to successfully teach students, one must know them, then there is no reason why we can't have one first-grade teacher per state, with each day's work being broadcast to hundreds of rooms filled with thousands of first-graders. The image is admittedly nightmarish, but it is the logical conclusion that stems from an embrace of technology as "delivery." We need to recognize that we can't go very far down that road before turning back becomes a practical impossibility.

There is another issue related to technology that I would like to briefly discuss. Because of our cultural assumptions about the superiority of urban over rural, rural educators have often been on the defensive. When telecommunications technology made it possible to "pipe in" televised courses, many rural defenders jumped on the bandwagon, saying, "Now we can offer as many electives as the big schools." Although I don't mean to suggest that televised courses should be scrapped—for I think this can be a beneficial option in exceptional cases—I do wish to suggest that there is nothing about urban or suburban schooling in this country that is worth emulating in rural areas. In fact, we ought to recognize that these places have begun to emulate rural schools by embracing such ideas as "less is more" and "schools within schools" (to make their educative operations small).

The movement of technology related to the improvement of schooling loses a great deal of momentum when one looks away from the educational enterprise construed as the provision of means for the economic market and instead embraces the conception of schooling for the cultivation of civic virtue. Millions of Americans use computer technology on a day-to-day basis without the benefit of any formal computer instruction in public schools. Math majors graduate from universities every year without having had the benefit of calculus in their high-school curriculum.

Having made the point, let me add, quickly, that there is nothing wrong with technology in rural schools; there is nothing wrong with giving rural students access to E-mail and the Internet. But we should not assume that dramatically increasing the amount of information available to students somehow translates into increased learning or deep-level understanding. As the constructivists tell us, new information is just one ingredient in the process of learning; but without the interplay of cultural assumptions raised to the level of consciousness and without give and take in making sense out of past experiences relative to cultural assumptions and new information, *understanding* is not going to occur. This suggests that learning is a profoundly social endeavor and that although technology can play a role in the process, it will never be more than a tool to be used in some instances and to be ignored in others. It is not a panacea. A living human being, called a teacher, is still required. As Neil Postman put it, "I know a false god when I see one."

The question regarding technology for rural schools, ultimately, will be this: What is appropriate given the context, the particular place on earth? All schools interested in the revitalization agenda will have to work this answer out for themselves. Technology is just one of many issues that will surface in conversations related to school change. Many places will not get beyond the conversation stage. Those that do, however, may be interested in concrete examples of what happens in the classrooms of schools that attend to their place. This is the focus of the final two chapters of this book.

8

Place-Conscious Elementary Classrooms

It is a great error to suppose that people are rendered stupid by remaining always in the same place.

—*William Cobbett, 1830*

What do you want to be when you grow up?" This question may be asked in elementary schools more often than any other. From very early on, children are socialized into an orientation toward the future. As I noted earlier in the book, we have given this particular orientation the cultural stamp of approval, whereas an orientation to the past gets a clear thumbs-down. There is no profound wisdom here, no natural law or innate prewiring at work. This is purely a cultural phenomenon that can be tied to a broad range of ingredients that have gone into the modern liberal recipe for selfhood.

As noted in earlier chapters, our political, economic, and educational theory since the Enlightenment has focused on the individual.[1] "We are all unique," we are ceaselessly told, just as we begin twelve years of institutionalized life that demands a most unforgiving brand of conformity. From day one on, children are encouraged to look to the future, and in the process, they are left with the message that their worth is wrapped up in their occupational choice (or, to put it a bit more maliciously, their occupational destiny) and that this worth has nothing to do with the depth and quality of the commitments they make in life. There are serious psychological ramifications here, because, as discussed earlier, deriving meaning from life seems to be inextricably tied to the quality of the commitments one makes and honors. Ignoring this completely, schooling in this culture is endowed with a certain instrumentality. That is, it has become the vehicle designed to transport kids to their future jobs. In direct opposition to John Dewey's plea that schools should not be preparation for life, but instead should be life itself, schools have plunged ahead with the idea that time "spent" in schools should prepare students for a job at some future point in time. This instrumentality has become even more refined and pronounced as the twentieth century has progressed. Increasingly, schools are viewed as the mechanism designed to give the corporate liberal state what it needs: workers capable of doing their jobs well and a certain elite group of math-science performers who will carry the torch toward American domination in the global economic market.

"If you want to be a chemist you'd better do well in math and science." Some variant of this statement is uttered thousands of times each year all across the United States, and on the surface, it is true enough. But it betrays more of the cultural baggage that has put us in our current condition—that of a society with no facility for ethical deliberation, a society with no sense of place or community, a society, therefore, marked by unmatched levels of criminality and violence. Our culture converts the school into a sorting mechanism. Whereas some students receive the clear message that they are destined for interesting, high-paying careers, others come to see themselves as destined for the "world of work." In either case, we have, in the process, converted the notion of formal schooling into a kind of youth holding tank, a mechanism that serves to occupy our children until the economic utility of adulthood, or at least late adolescence, arrives. While in school, kids are encouraged to think about their future jobs. "Career education" and its contemporary variant "school to work" are two prominent slogans that have played a large role in creating these kinds of cultural messages. The problem is that the "world of work" to which these programs pay homage is not something that students will one day "join." It is something they will one day create. The students in our public schools are the future decision-makers in this country, if there is still any truth to the notion of a government of, for, and by the people. Our high-school graduates (and our dropouts, for that matter) are not, first and foremost, factory hands or dentists or professional baseball players. They are citizens living, ostensibly, in a democracy. What they deserve and must receive through schooling is an education conducive to the development of a sense of political efficacy and, coupled with this, a program of concerted community enculturation into the ethic of shouldering a responsible measure of civic virtue. Democracy can do nothing but erode in the absence of these measures. But the cultivation of civic virtue is not solely for the benefit of society, for it opens up, within individuals, the possibility of substantively addressing the void in meaning that marks so much of modern life.

This is not to say that the world of work has no place in the public-school curriculum. Certainly work is an important dimension of life and therefore ought to be a topic for extended study and deliberation in public schools. But this study should be linked to the school's primary role of educating citizens who live in a democracy. What characteristics should work possess? How available should it be? How should it be compensated for? What kinds of policies need to be in place to produce the answers to these questions? What does the past tell us about policy possibilities? What will our future resemble if society elects to operationalize the wrong answers to these questions?

Beginning at the elementary level, students must be socialized into the practice and habit of researching and deliberating answers to the questions that vex their communities *at the moment*. Schools can become places that live and work in the present, with no more attention paid to the past or future than the amount necessary to add substance and depth to students' increasingly complex understandings about the world and the place of their community within it.

Some scholars claim that all institutions and organizations in the very near future will rise or fall on the basis of their success *at educating* everyone connected to them.[2] Lifelong learning takes on more and more meaning with each passing year. Education is a serious business, and this ought to be a kind of first maxim for everything that happens in schools. In a democracy, determining the extent and quality of social justice is the rightful province of its citizens. Every issue that touches human lives in this society can be peeled back, as with an onion, to expose the heart of the matter—the extent and quality of social justice. This is not to suggest that schooling ought to be one long, ceaseless political debate. It does suggest, however, that at any point in time, a student should be able, if asked, to make the connection between ongoing work in the classroom or in the community and the issue of social justice.

The elementary school is a great place to begin the process of removing the instrumentality that currently defines the public-school experience. The question of what a child will be when he or she "grows up" ought to be downplayed. Even at grade-one level, students should be encouraged to live in the present, not in the future. It is what they are at the moment that matters, and students need to see, in the curriculum and pedagogy exhibited by caring, professional teachers, that it does matter. There is nothing quite so detrimental to the psychological health of school-age youth as the near-constant message that they are nothing until they get out of school. It is a very damaging socialization into the adult world. Knowing, as we do, that children are surrounded by such a message for years, there ought to be little cause for surprise at the extremely high levels of youthful experimentation with sex, drugs, and alcohol.

* * *

It is all well and good to talk about focusing on the present with elementary-age students, about developing civic virtue and a capacity for give-and-take deliberation. Sooner or later, the question of "discipline" barges into the conversation. Teachers are quick to explain that children are not overly endowed with the patience required for deliberation. Children don't innately "take turns" when speaking, and it is important to note that listening is not one of their strengths.

These circumstances have contributed to the evolution of two persistent images of the elementary-school teacher. The first is deeply connected to the past, to the one-room schoolmarm. The image is that of the autocrat, the maker and enforcer of classroom rules. The "switch" is the symbol of this image: Break the rules, and expect a lashing. Although corporal punishment was primarily a nineteenth-century phenomenon, it was a defining characteristic of public schools well into this century. Today, at the century's end, there are still autocratic teachers working, but the punishments they employ have become less physical.

There is no need to go into a lengthy critique of the use of punishments to achieve the desired classroom atmosphere. Such critiques have been around for decades, even centuries. The French philosopher Michel de Montaigne, for instance, railed against it during the 1500s.[3] That psychological damage accompanies the extensive use of punishment in elementary schools is almost conventional wisdom today. Good teachers seem to know, intuitively, that using punishments to achieve desired behaviors is not a strategy conducive to maximizing student learning. It structures in student resistance to the pedagogical efforts of the teacher. As that occurs, tension enters the very "feel" of the classroom.

The gradual rise of this understanding to the level of common sense has contributed to the development of another powerful image of the elementary-school teacher. This image, which seems close to being the opposite of the first, is of the warm, compassionate nurturer of children. This teacher, far from being ready to brandish a switch at a moment's notice, is full of praise and good feeling. The "happy face" is the symbol of this image.

Critiques of this stereotype are considerably less pervasive than are those of the teacher as disciplinarian, but they exist nonetheless. All elementary teachers should take a serious look at Alfie Kohn's *Punished by Rewards*.[4] With our ability to dole out praise, we inure students to being emotionally dependent, a practice that is heavily criticized by a growing number of teachers and professors. The external signifiers of "good" behavior—the happy faces, the stickers, the candy bars, and so forth—all serve to take the focus away from learning and put it squarely into the realm of giving the teacher what he or she wants.

Rewards and punishments, however, do not exhaust the list of possibilities for dealing with the high energy and immediacy of childhood. Forrest Gathercoal has worked through a disciplinary orientation that seeks to balance "student rights and responsibilities." He calls his approach "judicious discipline," and I will be borrowing from his work later in this chapter.[5] I was drawn to Gathercoal's work because part of the process of community restoration involves balancing this tension between rights and responsibilities. An overemphasis on individual rights destroys community (not to mention the environment), whereas creating the balance inherent in observing individual rights while shouldering responsibility builds community. If simultaneous renewal is the agenda, it makes sense to make use of such an approach to address the question of discipline in rural elementary schools.

There is a great deal of interest in the issue of discipline within our nation's public schools. Despite the fact that it seems obvious that discipline problems are heavily context-dependent, there are those who claim that some clever step-by-step process will solve all problems. There are also those who assert that there would be no problems if parents would do their job. (The implication seems to be that their "job" is to inculcate within their children a capacity for immediate and unquestioning submission to authority.) And there are those who claim that there would be no problems if teachers would do their job. (The implication seems to be that teacher quality is measured by the ability to manipulate the behavior of all the children in a classroom.)

None of this is helpful. First of all, the "sure-thing" discipline package is a veritable for-profit industry in this country, despite the fact that would-be entrepreneurs, often looking to maximize their own self-interest, can promise little or nothing by way of results. Second, the claim that poor parenting is at the root of our discipline problems is also chimerical. Certainly, our culture has defined what constitutes good parenting, and just as certainly, it is no secret that a significant portion of the parent population in this country does not measure up. In the case of the affluent, for example, children often become inconvenient, an obstacle to the ever-hotter pursuit of self-interest. Poor parents, in contrast, having been socialized to believe that their inability to successfully maximize their self-interest is due to some failing on their part, also believe that this same something will constrain the lives of their children. Blaming inappropriate classroom discipline on parents is a malicious sort of "blaming the victim." The victims, of course, are the children whose parents have both won and lost the race for self-interest. Last, the claim that teachers are to blame for our epidemic-level classroom discipline problems just doesn't hold up under scrutiny. Although it is true that there are many common pedagogical and curricular practices that fairly beg for student misbehavior (such as reducing the school day to an unending series of worksheets), it is also true that the sole motivation for teaching is to help students learn. How could such an agenda be construed as an invitation to unruly behavior?

If we want to be serious about the question of school discipline, looking for shortcomings in either parents or teachers represents a waste of time and energy. The shortcoming is embedded in our culture. It takes the form of a fetish for individual acquisition, a fetish that has guided the evolution of schooling to facilitate that end. "Here's what you need to know" is, all too often, what teaching has become. Three-year-olds, in all but the most isolated homes, have already been socialized to accept the role of student with dutiful passivity while an older sibling or neighbor spiels out information at a rapid clip. It is not just community and the environment that are destroyed by a culture that eschews moderation and pronounces ethical deliberation a waste of time; the possibility of meaningful education is destroyed as well.

If a year or two of concerted school and community planning were followed by a reduction of teacher-student contact hours to a maximum of four per day, however, significant gains might be made quickly. Not only would student behavior improve, but so too would the depth and quality of the understandings constructed by students. Making such a schedule change, however, must be accompanied by change in the definition of schooling as a teacher workplace. That is, a significant portion of the teacher's day would then be given over to intense, in-depth study. Shared readings, action research projects, discussions, team planning, and the like would all become a part of the teacher's day. In short, an intellectual dimension can be reinserted into the profession, and students, as they begin to actively engage curriculum made relevant by connections to their place on earth, can become the beneficiary.

There are those who will say that an intellectual embrace of the immediate locality cannot be sustained for long, that students will inevitably have to go back to studying decontextualized "stuff," stuff they "need to know" or "have to have" for some future date with destiny (or with the Educational Testing Service, although there are those who claim that this is one and the same). This is a seductive argument, of course, for it legitimates the status quo—one more good reason not to change a thing. But imagine for a moment that the immediate locale *was* the lens for disciplinary engagement in all schools across the country. Next, try to imagine that we wanted to change this circumstance, that we wanted to make it, in fact, today's agenda. Could we create a persuasive argument? We would have to contend that we must not ground concepts and ideas in the child's immediate surroundings, that we must instead do what we can to decontextualize curriculum, to make it artificial and detached from the everyday life of the child. Far from being persuasive, such an argument borders on the ridiculous, and yet this is exactly what is said between the lines whenever the idea that schools should focus on their place is criticized.

The idea of using the immediate locality as a lens for disciplinary engagement is, at a minimum, as old as Rousseau. More recently, John Dewey made similar arguments, and a host of twentieth-century educational theorists have followed his lead. Still, the idea remains countercultural, and as a result, it may be worthwhile to attempt to describe what it means to use the school's place as a curricular lens. Perhaps the biggest hurdle here is recognizing that curriculum is simply not synonymous with information. Although there is certainly a mass of information one might "acquire" concerning various subjects—for instance, the American Revolution, photosynthesis, musical tone and timbre, quadratic equations, or nineteenth-century American novels—unless this acquired information is used by students to construct understanding about the world as it currently exists for them, the time spent in acquisition will have been wasted.

The school's place allows educators to take what is artificial out of the schooling experience. For example, questions can be framed to connect remote events with today's time and place: What circumstances led to the American Revolution? Do any of these continue to trouble the residents in our rural county? Which ones? How can we find out? Did the American Revolution create new dilemmas? Do any of these continue to trouble the residents of our county? With skillful pedagogical guidance, the school's place allows children to develop the intellectual flexibility needed to see history as a force in their lives rather than as an exercise in the acquisition of names and dates. All of the traditional "subjects" can reap the same intellectual rewards through a focus on place; and they can be made more powerful by engaging the place with a multidisciplinary approach. The depression era can become a subject that painfully touched real lives—the lives of community elders who come into the school to share their childhood experiences. Excellent songs, like those written and performed by Woody Guthrie, can sharpen student insight into the complex social questions raised by the dire circumstances of that era. Excellent novels such as Lois Phillips Hudson's *The Bones of Plenty* or Steinbeck's *The Grapes of Wrath* speak poignantly to the human condition and can thereby enrich the historical understanding constructed by students. Mathematics can enable students to chronicle depression-era outmigration from their own community, and family histories can then bring life to identified numerical trends. Science can allow students to explore the physical conditions that create significant periods of drought as well as those conditions that follow in their wake.

In short, place allows educators to see the artificial nature of subject-area boundaries and understand how this Progressive Era attempt at maximizing efficiency, which ostensibly stems from specialization, has worked to undermine the quality of the educational experiences offered by the modern school.

* * *

Forrest Gathercoal advocates a judicious discipline that daily reminds students of the interplay between rights and responsibilities. This is first-rate socialization for a democracy. It will quickly sour and backfire, however, if responsibility is trivialized by the adults in the school community.

One of the great difficulties with the school experience in this country is that young children, equipped with a wide-eyed idealism and a tremendous endowment of faith in adults, will often go along with trivialized conceptions of responsibility in their willingness to please. They will willingly oblige such familiar requests as keeping their hands to themselves, keeping their line straight, not budging, becoming silent instantly, taking turns at the drinking fountain, and so forth. As students get older, however, many begin to reject what they take to be the arbitrary use of power. After all, they wonder one day, why must a line be straight? Slowly, they come to recognize that submission is asked for more often than anything else, and when this recognition comes, they display the expected deference more grudgingly. Sometimes as early as the fourth or fifth grade, students have learned, in fact, to give the silence demanded by teachers only when their acquiescence will be exchanged for minimal amounts of homework. Many researchers have documented this sad, though pervasive, classroom "compromise."[6]

To avoid this situation, the very opposite of socialization for silence must be cultivated. One of the greatest educational contributions an elementary teacher can make is to socialize students into recognizing that talk—more accurately, deliberation—is and must be a predictable and indispensable part of schooling.

Talk comes naturally to kids. But our unfortunate response has been to subdue it, to curtail it, to train kids to turn it off like a light switch. Until recently, we were convinced that learning required silence so that knowledge could be stored away unimpeded in the heads of our students. The recent work of constructivist theorists enables us to look at knowledge as something socially constructed, and with this understanding, we can see the sense in Deborah Meier's claim that "learning is mostly talking, teaching is mostly listening." Students require socialization to learn the skills of responsible, courteous, and conversational deliberation. This does not come easily. It takes lots of practice. It is, however, a key ingredient in the cultivation of civic virtue. It is worth far more than all the phonetic rules or arithmetic formulas that currently fill our textbooks.

The best way to achieve this sort of socialization is to make elementary explorations of subject matter a matter of inquiry. Answers should not be provided by the teacher or the textbook. Rather, they should be deliberated on and thereby constructed by students. The teacher acts as a guide by asking questions, by encouraging research, and by challenging the naive interpretations that elementary-age children inevitably produce.

This suggests that the typical room arrangement, in which the teacher's desk faces straight rows of student desks, ought to become the exception rather than the norm. This traditional configuration was designed to enable students to efficiently record information, and it had the added advantage of facilitating the quick enforcement of silence. If these are no longer the primary goals of the teaching process, then some other room configuration is required. Many elementary classrooms today utilize small groups of desks throughout the room, and this is certainly an improvement. Another configuration that is rare in public schools is the complete circle made out of all available desks. This configuration is conducive to deliberation. There is much to be said for using it as the norm or perhaps as a configuration to begin and end each school day. In between, of course, desks will have to be moved to accommodate a wide variety of learning activities.

Having suggested this, however, I would caution the reader against putting too much emphasis on how the desks are arranged. All things considered, it is a minor point. But it is not unimportant. Messages are sent by the way the classroom is laid out, whether we, as teachers, are conscious of these messages or not. In the case study that follows, I use a circle of twenty-two desks (it could easily be twenty-five, twenty-eight, or thirty-two, or whatever; I fear there are still places in this country where this many students are placed in one elementary classroom) to project an image of how a typical classroom might be changed. Now, for the purpose of providing concrete examples, I would like to build the image even further.

For instance, visualize a first-year third-grade teacher surveying the circle of twenty-two desks that he has just created. It is his first contract day, and the flurry of beginning-of-the-year in-service meetings is still a few hours away. The student desks are arranged. At one point in the circle, he has inserted a chair that will accommodate an adult; he knows that he will be a part of the circle. He has taken the large teacher's desk and fitted it into a corner where he will work when his students are not in the room. The walls and bulletin boards are bare, and he is not at all certain what he should do with them. In a few minutes, he will seek out the principal to reacquaint himself with the school's policies and procedures and to ask several questions regarding curricular issues and a host of other concerns that have kept him awake at night for the past several weeks. He is getting ready to teach.

Because he attended a rural university where the professors were serious about preparing teachers for rural schools, he has latched onto and become committed to certain principles. The first is that he believes knowledge is socially constructed and that his instructional practices, therefore, must include socializing his students into the habit of courteous conversation and deliberation. He will not function as the provider of answers; he will, rather, facilitate the sound construction of answers by his students. Because he believes the very idea of providing an education for the sake of the economy or the "marketplace" will ultimately limit, even hamper, the intellectual growth of his students (and constrain his own professional growth as well), he has decided he will work for a nobler, more substantive end. He will do what he can to help his students visualize and then attend to the needs of the community of which they are a part. The students' place on earth, in fact, will be central to all of his curricular and instructional efforts.

Our hypothetical teacher is wise enough to know that his agenda is atypical, even countercultural. In his conversations with the other elementary teachers, therefore, he has stuck to traditional topics: "What level of proficiency do you, as the fourth-grade teacher, expect in the area of mathematics?" and "You had this group last year; can you give me any advice?" He plans to share his agenda slowly and mostly through example.

By the time the first day of school arrives, he has prepared a folder in which he will keep selected pieces of work produced by his students. And he has prepared a record-keeping journal in which he will document classroom activities, the subject areas engaged within each of these, and notes for future reference regarding student progress. He knows the names of his students by heart, and he has laminated twenty-two name cards and taped each one to its own desk. Within these desks he has placed the traditional textbooks, those that were used the year before by his predecessor. He is uneasy about these books, however, mostly because of an insight he took away from his university studies.

Like many of his peers entering the teacher preparation program, he considered textbooks and curriculum to be essentially the same thing. He was almost startled by an essay he was asked to read for one of his first elementary-education classes. It was entitled "Seven Reasons Why Textbooks Cannot Make a Curriculum,"[7] and the discussion that followed in class the next day was even more enlightening. Through that discussion, he learned that what students learn is a secondary concern for publishing houses. Their first concern is the bottom line; that is, they publish textbooks for profit. He discovered, too, that when an occasional textbook is published with careful attention paid to possible learning as opposed to sales, it usually doesn't fare well, for such books pay scant attention to what might make the process of teaching easy for teachers. It is those textbooks that look as if they will minimize the work of teachers that sell the best. This was a hard lesson to swallow, but it left him skeptical of textbooks. Still, the thought of beginning his first school year without them produced more anxiety then he could handle, so he placed them inside the student desks, knowing that they would be there when he needed them. He figured the math text would be a good source of practice problems, and as far as reading was concerned, his plan was to periodically work one-on-one with his students, asking each of them to read selections from the district's basal series, while he kept careful records of the process.

Our teacher had been a part of more whole language versus skills debates in his teacher preparation program than he cared to recall. He approached these with interest, but without passion. He could see strengths and weaknesses on both sides of the issue. Now that the time had come for him to make a decision, he found that it was more his view of education's ultimate purpose that moved him in a certain direction than the persuasiveness of a particular theory of learning. The same was true for other issues, including assessment. He was determined to be what he and a few of his undergraduate colleagues jokingly referred to as a "pointless" teacher. That is, arbitrarily created and assigned points would not be a part of his assessment procedures. If education was to be made relevant, if it was to be a seamless part of life itself, the constant reduction of information to its lowest skill or lowest conceptual elements would have to be eliminated. A fan of Howard Gardner's work,[8] he was interested in assessing the sophistication of the understandings his students would produce. The idea that this could somehow be done by assigning points seemed hopelessly shallow.

When the twenty-two students filed into the room, it was not difficult to discern their surprise on seeing the circle of desks. They whispered quietly as they searched the laminated name cards in search of their places. Once seated, they listened somewhat anxiously as their teacher introduced himself. The feeling of surprise in the room was even greater when he began to speak about the U.S. Constitution, asking how many had heard of it, how many knew what it was, and so on. He encouraged individual students to vocalize their responses. The discussion turned to individual rights and when those rights might be fairly restricted in the interest of the group.

Taking Gathercoal's "judicious discipline" to heart, he spent a great deal of time making sure his students possessed reasonably sophisticated conceptions of rights and responsibilities. He asked them to write down all the rights they thought they possessed as U.S. citizens. He wrote many of these on the board. Next, he asked them to write down all the rights they thought they possessed at school. Although it was clear from their expressions that the students thought this was a strange beginning to the school year, they did their best to do as their teacher asked. After writing the second responses on the board, he encouraged his students to talk about the overlap and the fact that school is not a separate experience, something unconnected to "real life."

Many students were eager to answer his queries—so much so that they frequently shouted their responses. It was clear that he would have his work cut out for him if he was going to make this kind of deliberation a central feature of the classroom. He persevered, however, with gentle reminders that everyone could not talk at once. Gradually, by asking questions and soliciting responses, he felt comfortable that his students were grasping the wisdom undergirding the idea that individual rights must be balanced by attention to responsibility for the group. He was pleased to see that this flowed naturally into a discussion of rules for the classroom. He surprised his students once again when the subject turned to gum chewing. One student, eager to please, suggested that there ought to be a rule against chewing gum in their classroom. But when he asked how one student's right to chew gum might prove to be a problem for the group, no one could come up with any answers. After supplying a few of his own, for the sake of argument (that gum sometimes ended up under school desks or bubble blowing sometimes became a distraction), he indicated that if the students wanted to try it as a classroom rule, gum chewing would be allowed. He made it clear, however, that this rule, like all others, was subject to periodic review and revision.

After a recess break, the morning was spent constructing copies of the classroom rules. They were posted at the front and back of the room, and all the students signed both copies, in the process indicating that they would do their best to abide by the rules they had generated.

Sitting at his desk at 4:00 P.M. after his first full day with students, our teacher reasoned that although everything had not gone perfectly, he had made an important, reasonably successful first step at socializing his students into life in a democracy. They had been a part of the rule-creating process, and he knew that the students felt that it had been a special experience, a different kind of first day.

On day two, his students generated lists of the things that interested them the most, and these, too, went up on the walls. Furthermore, he took one list home with him and put it up on his bedroom wall. Beneath it, he hung a blank sheet of butcher paper on which he intended to make notes related to interests that were common, interests that were in some ways intellectually interdependent, interests that seemed to lend themselves to collaborative student work. Next to that, making a kind of triangle, he placed a shorthand, "at-a-glance" curriculum guide that captured the essence of what the district expected in terms of third-grade "content." In no time, he had drawn arrows that went from student interests to district curriculum to the butcher paper, and they served as the incubator for all of his creative ideas. He was determined that the lists the students created would become an integral part of everything he did during the school year.

On the first day of school, the walls of his classroom had been completely bare. He recognized the skeptical look when a teacher or two strolled in during one of the in-service days before the students arrived. Anticipating this reaction, he quickly explained that his plans were to use student work to decorate the room. After a week of school, in fact, there were plenty of things on the wall, but it was also becoming apparent that without some careful attention to this matter, the room could quickly take on a cluttered, displeasing appearance. Instead of taking things down and rearranging them, however, he decided to discuss it with the students. Corrective suggestions were offered, then written on the board, and then the students were turned loose to make the changes. It made a difference. From that point on, the question of how additions to the walls might affect the overall appearance of the room, shared as it was by everyone, became a topic for discussion and deliberation.

Initially, our teacher used the math texts in a fairly traditional manner, except that students were divided into heterogeneous groups and were allowed to help one another with their work. As his confidence grew, however, he took his first steps toward community-oriented curricular integration of a very holistic sort. Having first been divided into three inquiry groups, the entire class took a field trip to examine local plant life. They went to a vacant lot in town, to the school's football field, and to a nearby farm pasture. In each location, one of the groups inspected a 10"x10" plot. The number and kinds of plants within each plot were counted. The students cut samples of the different plants and were able, back in the classroom, to identify differences between grasses and various weeds. The analysis was basic but accurate. The students were intensely interested in their work.

Although he had not yet introduced fractions, multiplication, or division, our teacher found that the plot work presented a perfect opportunity to do so. He proposed a number of mathematical problems for the class to solve: If the three football-field plots contained three weeds each, how could we arrive at the total number of weeds? What would we do if we wanted to analyze smaller plots the next time? He encouraged the students to vocalize their responses to questions that allowed clear conceptions of these principles of arithmetic to emerge, all before any time was spent on rote memorization.

The plant study naturally led to the concept of palatability, and that, in turn, led to the concepts of carnivore and herbivore. One of the students had an older brother in Future Farmers of America (FFA), and our teacher encouraged him to invite his brother to speak to the class about differences in the nutritional value of various plants, including those found in their plots. Through this process, the students learned a great deal about how food animals are raised, because the guest speaker told the students that many grazing animals never have a chance to eat the plants discovered in the pasture plots. Many are raised in feedlots, he explained. This sparked a flurry of questions from the students, and the FFA member found himself describing the practices of large-scale beef feedlot and hog confinement operations. He spoke of the advantages in terms of producing large amounts of food relatively cheaply, but he also warned of the environmental concerns that shadow these operations—things like polluted air and water. Our teacher was proud of the insightful questions raised by the students.

As he lay in bed that night, he knew that he was beginning to live out the principles to which he had professed allegiance during his undergraduate studies. The community was at that moment debating the pros and cons of large feedlots, for there were rumors that negotiations were under way with local landowners and that the county zoning board would soon have to consider a proposal for the variances that would allow a large meatpacking corporation to create a huge feedlot near town. His students could be a part of this community deliberation.

Many discussions ensued throughout the week. It was finally decided that the class could help the community by producing a poll that would tap resident attitudes toward the possibility of a large feedlot near town. The teacher allowed the students to determine what questions would be asked, but he encouraged them to solicit the age and gender of each respondent. This way, the students would have a chance to mathematically manipulate the data they collected. The editor of the local weekly newspaper was asked to respond to the poll. He was so struck by what the third graders were doing that he decided to do a feature story on the project. He photographed a group of students poring over the poll results, and he interviewed several of them to relay their reactions to being a part of the project. As if this were not enough attention, a television station some fifty miles away picked up on the story in the local paper. A reporter and film crew spent the better part of one morning with the class, intent on producing a two-minute human-interest clip for the nightly news.

After only three months of teaching, our teacher had begun to develop a reputation for innovation and being able to generate excitement. Whereas the parents of his students seemed thrilled with what was going on, his efforts did not go over as well among his colleagues. Although he had developed what he took to be a very good relationship with a few teachers, he could not mistake the air of resentment that seemed to emanate from others. He knew that behind his back several colleagues talked openly about merely having "fun and games," when the students were supposed to be learning mathematics and reading and science, and so forth. He was hurt by these indirect, sometimes very subtle, complaints from his peers. Although he had originally thought that he had landed in a perfect place to teach, he sometimes found himself wondering if he might not fit in better at another school.

The matter bothered him enough to broach it with one of his former professors at Christmas break. The professor reminded him of the many seminar discussions, of which he had been a part, that had focused on school culture and on what happens when it experiences the forces of change. He was clearly a change force, which was exactly what the teacher education program had prepared him to be. If he were to leave, the professor explained, the culture would go on as before. And, in any case, the chances of finding a job in a school that would not exhibit the same dynamics were slim indeed. What the teacher needed to do, the professor surmised, was to learn to share and collaborate in an unpretentious, uncontentious way. He advised, "Be an advocate for a more cooperative culture within the school and among the teachers."

The message was far from comforting, but our teacher came away better equipped to see himself as a part of the school's future and with greater ability to withstand the slings and arrows directed at his unconventional practices. He would stay the course.

*   *   *

Although this story is hypothetical, it was pieced together from real incidents. It is obviously not a far-fetched story, for these kinds of learning activities occur in rural classrooms all across the country on a regular basis. Few *schools* have embraced these ideas, however. If such a learning experiment takes place in your neighborhood, it is most likely the result of the school's having secured the services of the right teacher. The educational power that could result from an entire school acting on shared principle is enormous indeed, but achieving this requires the arduous work described in the previous chapter. There are no radical ideas motivating community-oriented pedagogy such as this, just deep thinking about what education is for and how teachers can best facilitate the construction of significant student understanding. Such thinking leads to considering the matter of relevance as a crucial component of learning, and it also leads to recognition that reconstituting community on an educational foundation may well be our best available solution to the violent culture that follows an excessive emphasis on individualism.

St. Augustine, the great Catholic bishop of North Africa, recognized, as Roman culture was disintegrating around him, that a significant contribution to the Roman predicament had been the failure of Rome's educational system to encourage students to go beyond Roman cultural assumptions.[9] If we make the same mistake, we can hardly expect a different result.

9

Place-Conscious
Secondary Classrooms

Our present "leaders"—the people of wealth and power—do not know what it means to take a place seriously: to think it worthy, for its own sake, of love and study and careful work. They cannot take any place seriously because they must be ready at any moment, by the terms of power and wealth in the modern world, to destroy any place.

—Wendell Berry, 1991

I have a colleague approaching her retirement years who was born and raised on a farm in South Dakota. She attended school and church in a small community that has since lost its school and churches. I have heard her tell a childhood story a couple of times now, a story that I think says a lot about American culture. When she was a small girl, there was an enormous amount of farm tenancy in South Dakota (and across the trans-Mississippi West, generally). Pickup trucks and wagons loaded down with beds, dressers, and sometimes farm implements such as plows were a common springtime sight. Families on the move like this were on their way to another farm, where they hoped to find better rental terms, thus increasing their chances for farm ownership sometime in the future. My colleague was one of the fortunate ones. Her parents owned their farm, and thus she was always a spectator of the springtime moves, never a participant. She laughs about it now, but as a girl, she felt cheated out of the excitement that must have come with being on the move—with seeing new sights, eating at a restaurant in town, meeting new children at school. From a distance, it all seemed very exciting.

The cultural dynamic captured by this story has been discussed by many of this nation's leading agrarian spokespersons, including Marty Strange, Wes Jackson, and Wendell Berry. They tease it out this way: If there is a part of the American farmer that wants his neighbor's land, there is another part that wants a neighbor. If it is true that rural Americans have always had the itch to move on,[1] it is equally true that they have also had an inclination to say, "No further. This is the place." None of these spokespersons is naive enough to deny the fact that mobility is seductive or that the desire for ever more wealth can quickly become the first filter through which all of life's decisions pass. Their point is simply that there is nothing innate at work here and that if thirty thousand years of human history is not enough proof of this, then one can find plenty of contemporary counterexamples throughout the American countryside.

One of the contributions of this book, I hope, is that it will enable the reader to see that proclaiming one's own cultural habits and practices to be "human nature" is very shallow and unsophisticated. Although more than a half-century's worth of economic theory has made a virtue out of greed, for instance, it has not made it an innate human proclivity. In fact, as I have attempted to demonstrate here, the most damaging cultural assumptions at work today can be traced back only as far as the seventeenth century. In terms of human history, this is a mere blip on the screen. But we are still very much caught up in modern versions of what constitutes liberal politics, liberal economics, and liberal education; and we are still very much convinced that our ideas define circumstances across all humankind. Our ideas—our version of liberalism—celebrate mobility and greed and, over time, have created the circumstance Wendell Berry captured in the epigraph to this chapter. And just as in the state-dominated Roman schools near the end of the empire, American students in our own schools are obtaining almost no intellectual control over their own cultural assumptions. The pursuit of self-interest becomes, for our students, the basis for approaching all questions in life. As a consequence, they learn to stand ready to break any and all ties for the right job, the right phone call, even the right set of flirtatious exchanges.

It doesn't take a great deal of insight to recognize that there is a profound poverty here or to recognize that virtuous character is something bound to be in short supply within such a culture. The recent explosion of prison construction in this country ought to be evidence enough that this is indeed the case.

In many ways, this book is a plea for Americans to consider renewing their schools so that they begin to appeal to that other lingering (though often buried) cultural vestige in America, the part that wants a neighbor and the part that wants to settle down in a particular place and carve out a decent life. Such an educational agenda is a direct contribution to the restoration of community in this country, but it is also a contribution to community rebuilt upon an educational foundation. Schools must strive to become what Peter Senge calls "learning organizations," for the joy of learning, in and of itself (and particularly when infused with significance for the learner by sophisticated pedagogical attention to place), can be an important counterbalance to the seduction of mobility and ever more material accumulation. In the previous chapter, we glimpsed what an elementary classroom might look like when a teacher takes this idea to heart. In this chapter, I will try to create a similar image of a place-conscious secondary classroom.

*   *   *

Imagine, this time, a first-year social studies teacher sitting in her classroom on the first contract day. Nervousness is mixed with excitement as she reviews what appears to be a very difficult (though all-too-typical across the rural United States) schedule. She will teach during six of the eight periods, the seventh will constitute her "prep" period, and during the last period of the day, she will monitor a study hall. She is responsible for teaching one section of seventh-grade U.S. history, one section of eighth-grade geography, one section of ninth-grade civics, two sections of tenth-grade U.S. history, and one section of twelfth-grade psychology. Over and above this, she will coach seventh- and eighth-grade girls' basketball, and in the spring, she will serve as the assistant to the varsity track coach. For fulfilling these duties, her district has agreed to pay her $19,000.

To a university professor in this country, such a teaching load appears appalling, unthinkable. It is not that university professors are lazy or reticent when it comes to work. Indeed, popular, albeit ill-researched diatribes against higher education notwithstanding, the literature is quite clear about the fact that the American professoriate works hard and for long hours. But the load described above is simply not conducive to intellectual growth on the part of the teacher—a circumstance that can only have a negative effect on students over the long haul. A large part of the reason that higher education in the United States is the clear world leader is that the education system here evolved as the very epitome of a learning organization. All of the traditions that surround higher education—discussions of shared topics, disciplined inquiry, blind peer-review—evolved from the highest value being placed on learning. It is true, however, that in recent years, power and profit have emerged as values to compete with learning as the heart and soul of the university experience. There are abuses, for instance, in the area of intercollegiate athletics, that are clear to everyone—but there are even more insidious abuses in the area of research for hire, of professors doing the bidding of multinational corporations and receiving university accolades because they "brought in grants."[2] These problems aside, however, the university is still our best example of a learning organization, and we should recognize that a professor's reaction to the common load shouldered by rural teachers across this country is simply that such a demanding schedule is not conducive to growth, nor could anyone make a defensible argument that it might be.

Whereas the elementary teacher typically has some room to work with the structural problems that impede teacher and student learning, conditions are generally tougher for the secondary teacher. Take our imaginary social studies teacher, for instance. Instead of twenty-two students, she has 170. Instead of some flexibility with regard to time, bells will chase students in and out of her room every fifty minutes. Instead of having the freedom to capitalize on topics that lend themselves to interdisciplinary study, she will operate in an environment where everyone expects her to honor disciplinary boundaries. As the old saying goes, she is expected to teach "subjects," not kids.

Our teacher, however, attended the same rural university as her elementary colleague described in Chapter 8. She has been prepared to approach her profession as an intellectual, rather than a technical, endeavor. She knows that the road ahead will be difficult, but she also knows why. That is, she knows enough about the history of education in this society to understand why so many structural obstacles lie before her. Far from being daunted by this knowledge, it invigorates her. Understanding the connection between the predominance of commercialist, urban-oriented policy and the problems of rural people and their communities has left her morally outraged. She can still recall the insight revealed by the renowned sociologist C. Wright Mills, an insight she encountered in one of her first education classes: "Personal troubles" cannot be differentiated from "public issues."[3]

Like her elementary counterpart, our social studies teacher has worried, prior to the start of the school year, about the matter of discipline in her classroom. She knows that prior socialization into passivity, into silence upon demand, will likely complicate her plans for a conversational, dialogical classroom. She knows from many hours of school observations in her teacher preparation program that her older students will not readily engage in substantive conversations, that they will prefer to keep quiet and look bored. She knows, too, that her younger students will read her approach as a chance to cut loose and act up—not ideal circumstances by any stretch of the imagination. But from her perspective, there are only two rational responses to bad odds: quit or try hard. Given the moral imperatives she sees embedded in a life dedicated to rural education, quitting is out of the question.

The circle of desks strikes her secondary students as just as much of a puzzle as it did the elementary students described in the previous chapter. The conversation dedicated to the Constitution, to the balance of rights with responsibilities, to the democratic creation, signing, and posting of classroom rules all went over reasonably well, although it was clear, particularly among her younger students, that the day would come soon when the rules would either have to be enforced or be deemed ineffectual.

Her chief difficulty was obvious before the first week was out: Her students didn't like to read. Part of the difficulty, she knew, was that the textbooks were mere compendiums of bland information, despite the fact that great effort had gone into making them provocative by inserting large colorful pictures or little "asides"—vignettes that might provoke some interest, though not enough to compel a student to wade through the rest of the assembled "stuff."

Less than three weeks into the semester, she began to understand what her professors had meant by "inquiry-based learning." Her answer to this "hot topic" was going to be special "projects" interspersed throughout the year. She began the year with the heavy use of textbooks (partially, she admitted to herself, for the safety-blanket effect—there is always plenty to keep students busy in a six-hundred-page book filled with hundreds of questions asking for factual recall); but then she began to see that there was no inquiry involved in what she was doing. She was not facilitating the construction of understanding; she was orchestrating the acquisition of information—and not being very successful at that.

At thirty-eight students—too many for one section—the tenth-grade class was the largest in the high school. Since she had one section of eighteen and another of twenty and because history had been her best subject in high school and college, she decided to use her sophomores as guinea pigs as she attempted to wean herself away from the use of textbooks. She divided each section into groups of four, after deciding on these four critical questions concerning the revolutionary era in American history:

1. What were the causes of the American Revolution?
2. What were the determining factors that resulted in an American victory in the conflict?
3. What were the key questions to be answered by the victorious colonies, and what does history suggest those answers were?
4. What were the causes of the Constitutional Convention, and how did the Constitution address the concerns that led to the convention?

She knew that the textbook devoted five succinct paragraphs to the causes of the American Revolution, but she also knew that telling her students to read them, remember them, and identify them when they were embedded in multiple-choice questions was not going to go anywhere toward building historical understanding.

Each group was assigned one of the questions she had developed and was given three weeks to prepare a position paper in answer to it. She worked with the principal to schedule a time when they could use the auditorium for a miniconference and debate. The two sections would come together to deliver their position papers and, after the public hearing, defend them. The students working on questions two, three, and four would be coached to probe the first group with questions—especially when differences in interpretation between the two sections became obvious. The groups working on the other questions would each take their turn on stage.

She encouraged the students to prepare visual aids to enhance the effectiveness of their arguments relative to their question. Many groups took the work very seriously and were actively seeking more information than either their textbooks or the school library could offer. Our teacher asked the custodian if there were any bookshelves hidden anywhere that she could use if she brought her own professional library into her classroom. The custodian responded by building makeshift shelves with boards and cinder blocks.

She had learned enough about cooperative learning in her teacher preparation program to know that there are problems with the approach that require thoughtful attention. She knew, for instance, that in some groups, one or two people might slack off, leaving one or two others to carry the bulk of the burden. She knew that some groups might spend more time discussing the past weekend rather than events at the end of the eighteenth century. Her response was to set up individual conferences with students once each week. She planned to hold their conferences before school, after school, and during her prep period. These would merely be brief conversations about the student's contributions to the group effort and a discussion of what the student was learning. She explained to the students that these meetings were important and that she would take extensive notes concerning the conversation. Also, each class period would end with four daily progress reports, one from each group.

Things worked relatively well. The students were happy with the format change, and they seemed to work hard on their questions. Our teacher found it very satisfying to be prompting the groups with questions that would push their analysis deeper, rather than simply filling up the overhead projector with names and dates.

When one student asked if her mother could come and watch the conference-debate, it sparked an idea that had not yet occurred to our teacher. Why couldn't they open this up to the general public? In no time, the students had created posters announcing the event and had placed them in the windows of downtown businesses. Additionally, a short announcement went into the newspaper. Expanding the audience in this way seemed to invigorate student effort. Several groups reported that they had decided to redo a few of their visual aids, aiming for a more positive effect on the audience. Others reported that they had heard that their counterparts in the other section were contending that such and such was the right interpretation and that they were working on ways to refute that position.

It wasn't perfect, and the groups weren't always on top of things, but our teacher felt good about what was happening. The students were excited, and they were putting in a lot of out-of-class hours to make sure the miniconference went over well.

When the big day came, two tables were placed on stage. Each one had a microphone that could be slid from one team participant to another. Additionally, a microphone was placed in the audience so that people could ask questions of each team. The event, which lasted two hours, was captured on videotape. There were a few visitors who decided to take in the event, perhaps fifteen or twenty in all. The seventh-grade U.S. history class attended as well, making the size of the audience seem much larger. Each question was an occasion for some disagreement between the teams. Once or twice the exchanges even became heated, and though the teacher had to intervene in these instances and had to bridge a few momentary lulls when no one seemed to have a question to ask, she felt as if she was really "in the background" and that the students had genuinely taken control of their own learning.

She had prepared a peer assessment form, which the students completed the day after the miniconference. Each group was rated by each of the nonparticipants as having exhibited exemplary, above average, average, below average, or unacceptably minimal understanding of its topic. Still, she was uneasy about what might have occurred in terms of across-the-board understanding. For instance, had the group working on the Constitutional Convention learned anything about the causes of the Revolution? She knew she could orchestrate a large group discussion that would give her some insight into this question, but she decided to do something else as an experiment. She had recorded the grades from three chapter tests in her grade book at that point in the semester, and she decided to give a fourth test, unannounced. It was the textbook series test accompanying the chapter dealing with the American Revolution. When the students grumbled as she handed it out, she fought back the urge to tell them it wouldn't count in their grade. She wanted her students to try their hardest so she could make a useful comparison. She averaged the first three series for each individual so that she could compare that score with the score on the unannounced fourth test.

She knew there were bits of isolated information on the exam that several groups would have dismissed as unrelated to their central concern. Because of this, she was surprised to discover that all but five students outscored their average from the first three tests. She immediately set up appointments with these students so that she could assess their understanding more accurately. In each case, she came away satisfied that these students had actually constructed a much more sophisticated understanding of the revolutionary experience than they had for the precolonial and colonial topics studied previously. Her first stab at inquiry-based pedagogy had worked. Not perfectly, perhaps, but it had worked.

During the evening after the miniconference, she worked up questions to guide her tenth graders through an examination of the Jeffersonian and Jacksonian eras. The bulk of her thoughts was shifting, however, to her seniors. She had grown to like several of these students, and she knew that despite the fact that there were thirty large bodies in the room, she could successfully employ a non-textbook approach there as well. In their text, the seniors were nearing the fourth chapter, "Intelligence Testing," and by fits and starts, she was piecing together what she hoped would be an exciting unit plan.

Her first step was to take advantage of her growing friendship with the fourth-grade teacher. She asked if her seniors might periodically work with the fourth graders in an experiment dealing with intelligence. Having assured the fourth-grade teacher that there would be no comparisons made and no scores given or recorded, she received permission to take the fourth-grade class, three times a week for two weeks. She planned to bring the fourth graders to the cafeteria during the fifty-minute sixth period during which her senior psychology class met.

She divided her thirty seniors into five groups of six each and explained to them that during the next three weeks they were going to study the concept of intelligence in depth and that, in fact, they were going to engage in a systematic attempt to measure intelligence. Each group was assigned a component of what is commonly assumed to constitute intelligence: verbal, numerical, analytical, reading, and creative abilities.

She used the textbook just long enough for the students to see how IQ tests were created and to study the formula used for generating an intelligence quotient. Next, she asked the students to break into the five groups and begin constructing test items that they thought would be appropriate for the fourth-grade level. She told them that they were in search of items that about one-half of the fourth graders were getting right and the other half was getting wrong. The students examined many tests that their teacher brought into class, everything from old standardized exams to tests in *Barron's Guide to the GRE*. When each group had a battery of twenty items, the groups went down to the cafeteria, where the twenty-five fourth graders were to be tested. Most groups discovered, within their first fifty-minute period, that they had under- or overestimated the ability of fourth graders. Few of these first items made it to the final round. After five more working sessions with the fourth graders, however, each group felt reasonably comfortable about having ten items that were at the right level of difficulty.

Although this hadn't been in her original plan, our teacher decided that her students needed the opportunity to try out their newly prepared intelligence test. She told her principal about what she was doing and what she wanted to do. She needed a group of fourth graders from another community, she explained, so that her students could administer their IQ test. She asked if he would contact a principal somewhere in the area who might cooperate. She explained that no names were needed, that the fourth-grade teacher would need to simply assign each student a number that included the sex and age of the student; for example, M1–10.2 would stand for male student number one, ten years and two months old. The students would have these numbers pinned to their shirts. The psychology class would set up in the school library and would work each student through all five sections of the test as efficiently as possible. After analyzing their data back in the classroom, the seniors would send intelligence "profiles," complete with IQ scores, to the fourth-grade teacher at their host school.

The principal successfully arranged the trip for the psychology class, and the experience proved to be better than the teacher had hoped. It was wonderful to see her football stars, boys who prided themselves on being tough, work gently and courteously with young children.

Back in their own classroom, the groups cooperated on calculating the IQ scores. Our teacher was unprepared for the resulting explosion of protest. Many of her students complained, "There's no way that this is accurate."

"Yes," the teacher said. "I already explained that our norming sample is too small."

"No, that's not it," another added. "This wouldn't be accurate if the sample had been in the millions."

"Why not?"

"Because it is more complicated than this. You can't just put a number on a bunch of right and wrong answers and call it intelligence."

"It's not intelligence, per se," the teacher responded. "It's a measure of how much intelligence exists." At this remark, the uproar grew even louder.

Before the class period ended, the students agreed to go through with their end of the bargain. Intelligence quotients, along with profiles identifying areas of strengths and weaknesses, would be sent to the fourth-grade teacher who had graciously allowed them to work with her students. But when this part of the project was completed, the class would spend more time studying intelligence testing and theories related to intelligence. Our teacher made copies of excellent work dealing with the history of intelligence testing, such as portions of Stephen Gould's *The Mismeasure of Man*. They also read parts of Howard Gardner's work[4] dealing with the theory of multiple intelligences. Last, they had several discussions related to the evolution of the Educational Testing Service and the role it plays, both positive and negative, in a society that professes allegiance to democracy.

Because many seniors were about to take a college admissions test, the discussion was immediately relevant. The teacher was able to ask about the likely college destination of someone with extraordinarily high scores and then about the likely occupational destination of that person once college was completed. The answers were predictable. The high scorers would go to Harvard and then to Wall Street.

There was clearly no better time to encourage the students to analyze this circumstance. "Is this kind of societal mobility beneficial to American society? Clearly, we encourage this now, but should we continue to encourage it?" Of course, many students were staunch defenders of the status quo. The chance for the high test-scorer to go to Harvard and on to Wall Street was what freedom was all about. The teacher reminded the students of their earlier serious critique of such test scores and then asked, "What about the freedom to stay in one's home community and lead an interesting life with an interesting job and a decent income? Where is that freedom?"

Several students began to criticize the culturally approved path to "success," though many others remained steadfast defenders of the status quo. This was not particularly troublesome for our teacher, for she knew she had accomplished something very difficult. An eminently powerful cultural assumption had been challenged by her students. The status quo defenders were there to witness it, and she knew that the next time this occurred they would be just a bit more likely to give serious consideration to the alternative. In short, she knew that she was playing a truly educative role.

With slow strides, her seventh-grade history class was becoming more discussion oriented. She found herself asking her students to interpret questions more and more, and she refused to entertain answers unless the students could support them with historical evidence. She decided to periodically collect written student interpretations of key events, such as the Monroe Doctrine, and place them in folders. They would be available to show to parents at conference time, and they would make good points of departure for discussions when the seventh graders entered her tenth-grade history class.

Because she was appalled at the writing skills of her seventh graders, she left the textbook tests behind and shifted to essay exams. This was not popular with the students, but it gave them an opportunity to gain experience at creating a particular intellectual position and supporting it. Once the class had worked its way into the nineteenth century, her approach to the study of history became very locally oriented. She asked questions such as these: "What Indian groups occupied this place before our ancestors came? What kinds of lives did they lead? Why?" The seventh graders researched the answers to these questions. They produced drawings of Indian tools and scale models of Indian housing. All of these things became decorations for the classroom.

An uncle of one of her students was a "black powder" enthusiast and regularly attended "fur-trading rendezvous," for which the participants dressed in full nineteenth-century regalia. The teacher made arrangements for this man to visit the class to help them learn about early white contact with the Native Americans in the area. Needless to say, this was a big hit with the students. Later, the class received an invitation to visit the farm on which one of the students lived. The parents of this particular student used horses for several farm chores, and our teacher decided that the farm trip might give her students insight into the difficulties experienced by the first couple of generations that had lived in their community. The students watched as the horses were harnessed and driven by an experienced teamster. They could see that driving a team was not as easy as it looked on television.

The trip was partly social, as they used the opportunity for a wonderful fall hayride, but it nevertheless sparked a great deal of interest in local history. In class, they discussed what the community must have been like when horses were the only means of local transportation and agricultural cultivation. "The town would need harness makers," the students surmised, "and blacksmiths for shoeing." The teacher asked how many businesses they thought their little community had once supported. Since their guesses varied wildly, she told them that it was going to be their job to find out. She asked her students to get in touch with the older residents of the community, to record their recollections, and, most important, to see if there might be photos that the class could use.

She was surprised to discover that there were many community photos in the homes of various residents, but most prospective donors were concerned about how the photos would be treated and in what shape they would be returned if they were temporarily loaned to a seventh grader. She discussed this with the principal, and they decided together to send an official letter to those residents who had indicated that they had early community photos. The letter would explain that the photos would be videotaped and then returned promptly and in perfect condition.

The letter had the desired effect, and soon they had more photos than they knew what to do with. The seventh-grade class worked quickly to identify and date the buildings in the photos and to put the entire collection in an order that made sense chronologically but would not impede the speedy return of the photos to their owners.

One of the seniors from the teacher's psychology class orchestrated an after-hours video project. After that, all that was left to do was to dub in a narrative history of the community and the many businesses that had once existed there. When this was done, the tape was brought to the local bank, where patrons could sit and view the pictorial history the seventh graders had assembled.

Satisfied that they had done something truly meaningful, the class was all ears when the students returned to their large circle. They were eager to hear about what was to come next. Our teacher, however, was not quite finished with their community history. She asked, "Why are there so few businesses now?" Many responses followed. All seemed to generally agree that it was too bad that so few existed now, but they also seemed to possess that fatalism that has become a part of our culture when they responded: "It is too bad, but it cannot be helped."

One student explained that the reason so many businesses had existed previously was that there had been so many farmers who needed services like those of the blacksmiths and harness makers. And the teacher then asked, "Why are there so few farmers today?" The student replied, "Because now there are big tractors that can work a lot more land than teams of horses." The teacher responded, "If we would like to have an interesting, active community, then, it seems like we should go back to horse farming." The student quickly rejoined, "But then there wouldn't be enough food to feed everybody."

"Do you have evidence to support this claim?" asked the teacher. "Because I am prepared to supply you with the results of a research study that show that your assertion is wrong." She explained to her seventh graders that she was not advocating a wholesale return to draft-horse farming; instead, she wanted to demonstrate that history is a record of choices made and that the choices that have affected their community have evidenced no concern for its health or vitality whatsoever. For good measure, she added, "In my view, this is not the way democracy is supposed to work."

Once again, she had reached a point with her students when she could tell that they were thinking beyond the bounds of cultural convention. She was providing an education. She knew that if rural America was to survive, let alone thrive, this kind of educational approach was going to have to become large scale.

She had a few friends at her school, but she knew that they were not doing the kinds of things she was. She felt some consolation, however, from the fact that her alma mater was producing teachers who were cognizant of the ends they would serve. But by Christmas, she knew that neither she, nor any of her colleagues from the university, would have an easy go of it. She knew that she was a good teacher, that she would continue to get better, and that she had already earned a healthy amount of respect from her students. For all of this, though, she seemed to receive a very lukewarm reception from her faculty colleagues. She knew that some of her colleagues were envious, and that didn't bring out the best in them. She rarely said much at faculty meetings, but when she did, the same two or three individuals could be counted on to dismiss what she had to say in short order. Although this troubled her, she didn't have much time to dwell on it. Her teaching days had become whirlwinds of activity. By Christmas, she could already think back on the tinge of nervousness she used to feel when twenty minutes were left in the period, her presentation was over, and she was wondering if her students would attend to their homework or get out of control while ignoring it. Such worries seemed slightly amusing to her now.

*   *   *

Once again, this hypothetical description is more real than imagined. There is nothing described here that hasn't happened or isn't happening on a regular basis in various places across the country. Imagine the results, though, if an entire school began to move in this direction, if teams of teachers engaged the immediate locality as a curricular lens. The school would begin to take on a different feel, and the community would experience a sense of reinvigoration, which, for many places, would be the first such experience in decades.

Skeptics will still point to "the tests" on which students must perform well in order to gain college admission and say we can't change because of those tests. The irony here is that an active pedagogy of place results in greater wherewithal for success on these exams because, if done well, it results in tested content that is understood rather than temporarily acquired.

Furthermore, of course, unlike their Roman counterparts more than a millennium ago, these students will develop the intellectual understanding necessary to see their immediate circumstances for what they are: a reflection of the quality of social justice in this society. It is a sure bet that if strengthening communities is indeed a part of the antidote to our most serious societal problems, creating schools dedicated to this goal is a step in the right direction.

If students have been enculturated into an ethic of shouldering responsibility for a shared place, into reasoned study and deliberation, and into a propensity to look beyond conventional wisdom for solutions to problems, that will certainly increase the odds that community will become a primary factor in our economic and political reckoning in the future. Working toward this end gives us the right to expect more than the prisons, the violence, the abuse, and the poverty—and the simultaneous decadent affluence at the other end of the spectrum—that have come to define American society.

Conclusion

I have watched a butterfly make its flight against a gale, and the performance gives me hope. If an insect can overcome such a monumental difficulty, surely humans are capable of solving their man-made problems.
—Norris Alfred, 1991

There is little doubt about the fact that the twentieth century will be seen as an extraordinary paradox. On the one hand, it has been a century marked by a veritable explosion in information and in tremendously complex technology, but on the other hand, it has been a century marked by profound ignorance.

The amount of wealth that has been spent on new and creative ways to kill and destroy is almost beyond measurement. The six million Jews who died in Germany have left an indelible mark on the entire century. The nuclear arms race is now widely viewed as the madness that it was. The extent to which we have permitted the unfettered exploitation of nature has rendered extended human existence on the planet a debatable proposition. The consolidation and control of the global food supply by a handful of multinational corporations represents another example of ignorance of the most profound sort. No previous age can possibly match this kind of large-scale stupidity.

It is not difficult to piece together the circumstances that have put us in our current situation. We have openly embraced a political theory that is fundamentally destructive of communities, and in the process, we have rendered the average citizens of the country politically impotent. Our economic theory has made a virtue of hedonism, and so another severe blow has been dealt to community in America. Regrettably, we have allowed our educational theory to trail behind politics and economics. Whatever agenda was set in those realms has been taken up and legitimated in the schools: If centralization and efficiency were good for politics and business, they were good for education as well. And so we have built schools large enough to accommodate thousands of students—another example of utter ignorance. Children, we now know and understand all too well, cannot thrive in the warehouses we have spent huge sums to build. All across the country, educators are taxing their creative energies to think of ways to alleviate the ramifications of egregious errors made in the past.

This is one more reason that rural areas are the most likely sites for the healing that must begin. They are small enough to be managed democratically and humanely. These places have the last best shot at restoring a sense of intradependence, at restoring time to the service of education (rather than the other way around), and at elevating a healthy respect for risk up to the status of cultural wisdom. We know now how community was eroded over time, and we know all too well how badly its restoration is needed. Unencumbered by the destructive ignorance set in motion during the industrial century, rural schools, as Part Three of this book has demonstrated, can begin the process of renewing their communities.

It is my sincere hope that the reader will join me in this effort.

Notes

Chapter One

1. Thomas Cahill, *How the Irish Saved Civilization* (New York: Doubleday, 1995), 39–40.

2. To be fair, in fact, one might argue that the inward or individualist turn in the dominant worldview was due more to the interpretation of St. Augustine advanced by later liberal thinkers, most notably Rousseau, rather than to Augustinian political theory itself. *The City of God*, for instance, does not ignore the polis. St. Augustine's inward search for the source of things, many claim, is merely an attempt to put himself at harmony with all things. It is, generally speaking, *The Confessions* that people point to when referring to St. Augustine the individualist. See Henry Paolucci, *The Political Writings of St. Augustine* (South Bend, Ind.: Gateway Editions, 1962).

3. John Rawls, *Political Liberalism* (New York: Columbia University Press, 1993), xxiv–xxvi.

4. Descartes' own words were actually "I am, I exist." The phrase "I think, therefore I am" was actually the work of a French translator of Descartes' *Discourse on Method*. Descartes accepted this translation, however. See Bernard Williams, *Descartes: The Project of Pure Enquiry* (New York: Penguin Books, 1978), 72–73.

5. Again, this is regrettably all too literal, although a century later Mary Wollstonecraft would have something to say, quite forcibly, about this. See her *A Vindication of the Rights of Women* (New York: Penguin Books, 1992; originally published in 1792).

6. René Descartes, *Discourse on Method* and *Meditations* (Indianapolis, Ind.: Bobbs-Merrill, 1960), 45.

7. Adam Smith, *The Theory of Moral Sentiments* (New Rochelle, N.Y.: Arlington House, 1969), 127.

8. The idea that individuals could pursue their passions and in the process generate the common good is a huge departure from medieval thinking about the inherent evils connected to "avarice and cupidity." Converting greed into a virtue was not accomplished overnight and certainly not by Adam Smith alone. Similar arguments were made by Montesquieu in France, Vico in Italy, Herder in Germany, and Mandeville (prior to Smith) in England. For an excellent discussion of this transition, see Albert O. Hirschman, *The Passions and the Interests: Political Arguments for Capitalism Before Its Triumph* (Princeton: Princeton University Press, 1977).

9. See, for instance, David Hogan, "The Market Revolution and Disciplinary Power: Joseph Lancaster and the Psychology of the Early Classroom System," *History of Education Quarterly* 29 (fall 1989):381–417.

10. Victor V. Magagna, *Communities of Grain: Rural Rebellion in Comparative Perspective* (Ithaca: Cornell University Press, 1991), 13–14. Magagna does an excellent job of chronicling all of the European and Third World studies that point to this place-community connection.

11. Intradependence captures the requirement of place as a dimension of community. Using the term "interdependence," i.e., meaning between individuals or between individuals and nature, tends to dichotomize or contractualize community relations and clearly fits with the technorationality of the Enlightenment project. There are always good reasons to reject interdependence. If in the Lockean tradition, for instance, "improvements" that put interdependence temporarily at hazard ultimately yield "tenfold benefits" for some larger economy or national interest, one can easily justify this.

Or through the accumulation of capital, one might simply cease to require the benefits of interdependence. The notion of *intra*dependence, however, recognizes that one acts upon "larger interests" by taking action within the place shared with others.

12. Probably the best argument made in this regard is Kenneth Jackson's *Crabgrass Frontier: The Suburbanization of the United States* (New York: Oxford University Press, 1985).

13. G. H. Sabine, "Beyond Ideology," *Philosophical Review* (January 1948):135.

14. This passage is quoted in Luc Ferry, *The New Ecological Order* (Chicago: University of Chicago Press, 1995), xv.

15. Philip Slater, *Earthwalk* (New York: Bantam Books, 1974), 233.

16. I am indebted to David Orr for the anthropological insights offered by Slater and Redfield. See Orr's *Earth in Mind: On Education, Environment, and the Human Prospect* (Washington, D.C.: Island Press, 1994), 193–194.

17. On this subject there is no better analysis available than John Berger's *Pig Earth* (New York: Pantheon Books, 1979).

18. See Carolyn Merchant, *The Death of Nature: Women, Ecology, and the Scientific Revolution* (San Francisco: Harper and Row, 1980), 46–47.

19. James A. Henretta, "Families and Farms: *Mentalité* in Pre-Industrial America," *William and Mary Quarterly*, 3d ser., 35 (1978):7.

20. Stephen Innes, "Land Tenancy and Social Order in Springfield, Massachusetts, 1652–1702," *William and Mary Quarterly*, 3d ser., 35 (1978):34.

21. Timothy Breen, "Persistent Localism: English Social Change and the Shaping of New England Institutions," *William and Mary Quarterly*, 3d ser., 32 (1975):7.

22. Henretta, "Families and Farms," 5.

23. Clarence H. Danhof, *Change in Agriculture: The Northern United States, 1820–1870* (Cambridge: Harvard University Press, 1969), 2.

24. The emphasis on the Midwest is a deliberate attempt to stay away from the need to engage the variable of slavery. Although I believe there are important lessons to be gleaned from this work for southern rural dwellers, the legacy of slavery has permanently altered the southern rural story. I recommend that interested readers take up the work of William A. Link, *A Hard Country and a Lonely Place:*

Schooling, Society, and Reform in Rural Virginia, 1870–1920 (Chapel Hill: University of North Carolina Press, 1986); James D. Anderson, *The Education of Blacks in the South, 1860–1935* (Chapel Hill: University of North Carolina Press, 1988); and Joe L. Kincheloe and William F. Pinar, *Curriculum as Social Psychoanalysis: The Significance of Place* (Albany: State University of New York Press, 1991).

25. Clinton Rossiter, ed., *The Federalist Papers* (New York: Mentor Books, 1961), 80.

26. Daniel Kemmis, *Community and the Politics of Place* (Norman: University of Oklahoma Press, 1990), 15.

27. In subsequent chapters we will take up the matter of education and agrarian liberal theory in a more complete manner.

28. "The Defects of the Irish," *Massachusetts Teacher* (October 1851):290.

29. Patricia Nelson Limerick, *The Conquest of the West* (New York: W. W. Norton, 1988); Richard White, *It's Your Misfortune and None of My Own: A New History of the American West* (Norman: University of Oklahoma Press, 1991).

30. This had significant ramifications. Philippe Aries argues in *Centuries of Childhood: A Social History of Family Life* (New York: Vintage Books, 1962) that there was no "childhood" concept in premodern Europe. This is perhaps related to the fact that life contained no divisions between "work" and "nonwork" as such, for this is clearly a major distinction today between childhood and adulthood. Certainly there were times during the feudal ages when people elected not to complete a particular chore and went off to a pub instead. But this is just the point. For the masses of people in the contemporary industrialized West, the decision to go off to the pub can take place only during hours officially designated as nonwork, or leisure hours. If I am right about this, and I believe I am, then the argument in Elizabeth Hampsten's *Settlers' Children: Growing Up on the Great Plains* (Norman: University of Oklahoma Press, 1991), where she compares parental dispositions toward children on the plains to the Aries thesis, is right on target.

31. John Mack Faragher, *Sugar Creek: Life on the Illinois Prairie* (New Haven: Yale University Press, 1986), 60.

32. It is often noted, for instance, that these states were the first to give women the right to vote. This is sometimes explained with the contention that women were so much more crucial to the western political economy than they were, apparently, to the eastern political economy that the westerners felt obliged to extend the franchise. I find this account remarkably unpersuasive. From my perspective it appears that women were always crucial to the stable functioning of society and that they were overworked and underappreciated in the East as well as in the West. It seems to me that both the democratic propensities of the western states and the fact that they decided to do something about the circumstances of women's lives (and in the realm of education one can see this clearly in their early decisions to provide free textbooks, allow women to vote in school elections and to serve as superintendents, and so on) are practices attributable to the circumstance that both the states and women were victims of undemocratic practices.

I have argued this in greater detail elsewhere; see Paul Theobald, *Call School: Rural Education in the Midwest to 1918* (Carbondale: Southern Illinois University Press, 1995).

33. Lawrence Goodwyn, *Democratic Promise: The Populist Moment in America* (New York: Oxford University Press, 1976). I should note here that the "trans-Mississippi West" includes Texas, Oklahoma, and to some degree Arkansas, each of which were the recipients of farmers excluded from older regions. Many of these new arrivals were African Americans and "poor whites" who were trying to escape the notorious "crop-lien" system established by the ex-planter class of the Old South. Many of the alliance's most prominent spokespersons were from these states.

34. See, for example, Marty Bender's work entitled "Industrial Versus Biological Traction on the Farm" in Wes Jackson, Wendell Berry, and Bruce Colman's *Meeting the Expectations of the Land: Essays in Sustainable Agricultural and Stewardship* (San Francisco: North Point Press, 1984), 87–105.

35. Merrill D. Peterson, ed., *Thomas Jefferson: Writings* (New York: Library of America, 1984), 5.

36. Clearly, many aboriginal groups around the globe established high degrees of intradependence. This was not universally the case, however, because these groups were sometimes forced to rely predominantly on sedentary agriculture, particularly irrigated agriculture.

Chapter Two

1. To say that farmers were not particularly excited about public schools in the first place is not to say they were not excited about schools. The farmers of the Midwest established their own schools before "free schooling" became the law of the land. Often these schools were connected to a local church, with classes frequently taught by clergy, but always with some kind of subscription fee attached.

"Subscription schools" served the needs of local farmers in ways that were less ideologically troublesome than the new tax-supported school system. See my history of rural education in the Midwest, *Call School: Rural Education in the Midwest to 1918* (Carbondale: Southern Illinois University Press, 1995).

2. Neil Postman, *Technopoly: The Surrender of Culture to Technology* (New York: Vintage Books, 1993).

3. Bede the Venerable, the eighth-century English monk, was responsible for beginning the dating system with "the year of our Lord," or *annus domini*. It was many centuries, however, before the European system was totally standardized. Medieval European merchants frequently transported themselves ahead and behind by years as they moved from one area of Europe to another. Although the Romans had adopted the twelve-month calendar, they divided it into unequal periods called the Kalends, Nones, and Ides. It took many centuries for them to arrive at a system where the number of days in each month was designated in ascending order.

4. Eviatar Zerubavel, *Hidden Rhythms: Schedules and Calendars in Social Life* (Chicago: University of Chicago Press, 1981), xii.

5. Kepler is quoted in Lewis Mumford, *The Myth of the Machine: The Pentagon of Power* (New York: Harcourt, Brace, Jovanovich, 1970), 86.

6. Zerubavel, *Hidden Rhythms*, 93–94. See also Marvin Minsky, *The Society of Mind* (New York: Simon and Schuster, 1986), 50–52, and Jeremy Rifkin, *The End of Work: The Decline of the Global Labor Force and the Dawn of the Post-Market Era* (New York: Putnam, 1995), 186–187.

7. Christopher Lasch, *The Culture of Narcissism: American Life in an Age of Diminishing Expectations* (New York: W. W. Norton and Company, 1978).

8. Wendell Berry, *What Are People For?* (San Francisco: North Point Press, 1990), 168.

Chapter Three

1. Robert Fulgham, *All I Really Need to Know I Learned in Kindergarten* (New York: Villard Books, 1989).

2. Risk is just one factor, and I believe, as I have said, that it may be of the most consequence.

There is also the "intellectual chaos" Ted Sizer speaks of, the near-constant labeling that goes on in schools (gifted, talented, disabled, and the like) and the uneven power dynamics that often border on clear authoritarianism. All of these circumstances promote indifference in the classroom.

3. Francis Bacon, *Novum Organum.*

4. There is debate, however, over what caused it. See, for example, Hilton L. Root, *Peasants and King in Burgundy: Agrarian Foundations of French Absolutism* (Berkeley: University of California Press, 1987), 1–21.

5. Herman Daly, "Introduction to the Steady-State Economy," in Daly, ed., *Economics, Ecology, Ethics* (San Francisco: W. H. Freeman, 1980), 19.

6. Paul Theobald and Ruben Donato, "Children of the Harvest: The Schooling of Dust-Bowl and Mexican Migrants During the Depression Era," *Peabody Journal of Education*, 67 (summer 1990):29–45.

7. Although this is a hypothetical example, the same scenario has played itself out hundreds of thousands of times in this country. For an excellent discussion of these dynamics, see Marty Strange, *Family Farming: A New Economic Vision* (Lincoln: University of Nebraska Press, 1988).

Chapter Four

1. James A. Montmarquet, *The Idea of Agrarianism: From Hunter-Gatherer to Agrarian Radical in Western Culture* (Moscow: University of Idaho Press, 1989), 69. Also, see Lynn White, *Medieval Technology and Social Change* (New York: Oxford University Press, 1969), 64–78.

2. Thomas More, *Utopia* (New York: Penguin Books, 1985), 46–47.

3. Quoted in W. E. Tate, *The Enclosure Movement* (New York: Walker and Company, 1967), 70.

4. Ibid., 135.

5. When England split from the Roman Catholic Church during the sixteenth century, the dissolution of lands that had belonged to various Catholic monasteries represented another window of opportunity that allowed some peasants to become landholders. But it was also an opportunity for the nobility and gentry to create quick, large-scale enclosures, forcing many of the peasants who worked the monastery lands to drift to cities in search of work. Whereas there was opportunity for some, there was also a good deal of hunger and suffering for others.

6. A.M.D. Hughes, *Cobbett Selections: With Hazlitt's Essay and Other Critical Estimates* (Oxford: Clarendon Press, 1923), 118. The reference to William Rufus is

made to dramatize the point since William Rufus, or William II, the son of William the Conqueror, king from 1087 until 1100, is said to have been one of the most ruthless and cruel monarchs in English history.

7. Isaiah Berlin, *Four Essays on Liberty* (Oxford: Oxford University Press, 1969), and C. B. Macpherson, *Democratic Theory: Essays in Retrieval* (Oxford: Oxford University Press, 1973).

8. R. H. Tawney, *The Agrarian Problem in the Sixteenth Century* (London: Longmans, Green, and Co., 1972), 46.

9. The clear differences between Hobbes' *Leviathan* and Winstanley's *The Law of Freedom* provide a sharp contrast between the political, economic, and educational options that were open to Cromwell and help make it clear that choice, rather than some kind of natural inevitability, was at work in shaping the eventual direction of liberalism.

For an in-depth exploration of this thesis, see Dale T. Snauwaert and Paul Theobald, "Two Liberal Trajectories of Civic Education: The Political and Educational Thought of Hobbes and Winstanley," *Journal of Educational Thought* 28 (August 1994):179–197.

10. D. M. Wolfe, *Leveller Manifestoes of the Puritan Revolution* (New York: Thomas Nelson and Sons, 1944), 71.

11. D. W. Petergorsky's *Left Wing Democracy in the English Civil War: A Study of the Social Philosophy of Gerrard Winstanley* (London: Victor Gollanez, 1945) is still, perhaps, the best treatment of the digger movement.

Christopher Hill's classic study, *The World Turned Upside Down: Radical Ideas During the English Revolution* (New York: Penguin Books, 1972), is also an important contribution to understanding what was at stake in this tumultuous time.

12. Gerrard Winstanley, *The Works of Gerrard Winstanley*, ed. G. H. Sabine (New York: Russell and Russell, 1965), 357.

13. Petergorsky, *Left Wing Democracy*, 145.

14. Winstanley, *Works*, 250.

15. Dale T. Snauwaert, *Democracy, Education, and Governance: A Developmental Conception* (Albany: State University of New York Press, 1993), 60.

16. Daniel Kemmis, "The Last Best Place: How Hardship and Limits Build Community," in Scott Walker, ed., *Changing Community* (St. Paul: Graywolf Press, 1995), 277–287.

17. John Locke, *Second Treatise on Government* (Indianapolis, Ind.: Hackett Publishing, 1980), chap. 5, par. 28.

18. There is debate about this point. James Montmarquet lays out the two sides of this debate clearly in his *The Idea of Agrarianism*, 80–82.

19. Locke, *Second Treatise*, 19.

20. Quoted in Jean Bethke Elshtain, *Democracy on Trial* (New York: Basic Books, 1995), 32–33.

21. The song "Me and Bobby McGee" was written by Kris Kristofferson, and this particular lyric nicely captures the shallow nature of a negative conception of freedom.

22. For these and further descriptions of the despicable conditions former peasants endured, see Kirkpatrick Sale's excellent book, *Rebels Against the Future: The Luddites and Their War on the Industrial Revolution* (Reading, Mass.: Addison-Wesley, 1995), 48.

23. Quoted in Montmarquet, *The Idea of Agrarianism,* 241.

24. Oliver Goldsmith, "The Deserted Village," in William Harmon, ed., *The Top 500 Poems* (New York: Columbia University Press, 1992), 342.

25. I described this process years ago in an article entitled "The Concept of Place in the New Sociology of Education," *Educational Foundations* 6 (1992):5–20.

Chapter Five

1. Merrill D. Peterson, ed., *Thomas Jefferson: Writings* (New York: Library of America, 1984), 290–291.

2. Thomas Paine, "Agrarian Justice," in *The Life and Works of Thomas Paine,* ed. by William M. Van der Weyde (New Rochelle, N.Y.: Thomas Paine National Historical Association, 1925), 10:9, 13, 15.

3. David P. Szatmary, *Shays' Rebellion: The Making of an Agrarian Insurrection* (Amherst: University of Massachusetts Press, 1980), xi–xiv.

4. Ibid., 45.

5. Ibid., 67.

6. Ibid., 69.

7. Thomas V. DiBacco, Lorna C. Mason, and Christian G. Appy, *History of the United States* (Boston: Houghton Mifflin Co., 1991), 114.

8. Ibid.

9. Szatmary, *Shays' Rebellion,* 131–133.

10. Peterson, *Thomas Jefferson: Writings,* 913, 917.

11. Jefferson is quoted in Daniel Kemmis, *Community and the Politics of Place* (Norman: University of Oklahoma Press, 1990), 11. Kemmis' words are from this page as well.

12. Dale T. Snauwaert and Paul Theobald, "Two Liberal Trajectories for Civic Education: The Political and Educational Thought of Hobbes and Winstanley," *Journal of Educational Thought* 28 (1994):179–197; and R. L. Greaves, "Gerrard Winstanley and Educational Reform in Puritan England," *British Journal of Educational Studies* 17 (1969):166–176.

13. David B. Tyack, "Forming the National Character: Paradox in the Educational Thought of the Revolutionary Generation," *Harvard Educational Review* 36 (1966):36; and Szatmary, *Shays' Rebellion,* 45.

14. Daniel M. Friedenberg, *Life, Liberty, and the Pursuit of Land: The Plunder of Early America* (New York: Prometheus Books, 1992), 359.

15. Ibid.

16. For these examples, see the popular high-school history text by John A. Garraty, *American History,* rev. ed. (Boston: Houghton Mifflin, 1986), 224.

17. See Gary Kulik's "Dams, Fish, and Farmers: Defense of Public Rights in Eighteenth-Century Rhode Island," in Steven Hahn and Jonathan Prude, eds., *The Countryside in the Age of Capitalist Transformation: Essays in the Social History of Rural America* (Chapel Hill: University of North Carolina Press, 1985), 25–50.

18. Wendell Berry, *A Continuous Harmony: Essays Cultural and Agricultural* (New York: Harcourt Brace Jovanovich, 1972), 162.

19. Henry David Thoreau, *Walden and Other Writings of Henry David Thoreau,* ed. Brooks Atkinson (New York: The Modern Library, 1967), 714.

20. Ralph Waldo Emerson, *The Works of Ralph Waldo Emerson,* comp. Edward Emerson (New York: Fireside Editions, 1898), 1:48.

21. Alexis de Tocqueville, *Democracy in America,* ed. Richard D. Heffner (New York: Mentor Books, 1956), 198.

22. Henry David Thoreau, *The Writings of Henry David Thoreau* (New York: AMS Press, 1968), 19:67.

23. Lawrence Cremin, ed., *The Republic and the School: Horace Mann and the Education of Free Man* (New York: Teachers College Press, 1957), 87.

24. See, for example, David B. Tyack, *The One Best System: A History of American Urban Education* (Cambridge: Harvard University Press, 1974), and Michael Katz, *The Irony of Early School Reform: Education in Mid-Nineteenth Century Massachusetts* (Boston: Beacon Press, 1968).

25. For a detailed account of the anatomy of rural resistance to public schools and public-school initiatives, see Paul Theobald, *Call School: Rural Education in the Midwest to 1918* (Carbondale: Southern Illinois University Press, 1995).

26. Emerson, *Works of Emerson,* 1:232.

27. Ibid., 7:134–135. Emerson's notion of small economies within a great economy is similar to a contemporary argument advanced by Wendell Berry in an essay entitled "Two Economies" in *Home Economics* (San Francisco: North Point Press, 1987), 54–75.

28. Theobald, *Call School,* 35.

29. See, for example, Allan Kulikoff, *The Agrarian Origins of American Capitalism* (Charlottesville: University Press of Virginia, 1992); Christopher Clark, *The Roots of Rural Capitalism: Western Massachusetts, 1780–1860* (Ithaca: Cornell University Press, 1990); Peter C. Mancall, *Valley of Opportunity: Economic Culture Along the Upper Susquehanna, 1700–1800* (Ithaca: Cornell University Press, 1991); and James A. Henretta, *The Origins of American Capitalism: Collected Essays* (Boston: Northeastern University Press, 1991).

30. John W. Adams and Alice B Kasakoff, "Migration and the Family in Colonial New England: The View from Genealogies," *Journal of Family History* 9 (1984):27.

31. Henretta, *Origins,* 79, 81.

32. Theobald, *Call School,* 34.

33. Mancall, *Valley of Opportunity,* 236.

34. John Mack Faragher, *Sugar Creek: Life on the Illinois Prairie* (New Haven: Yale University Press, 1985), 145.

35. Henretta, *Origins,* 81.

36. Faragher, *Sugar Creek,* 237.

37. Uffe Ostergaard, "Peasants and Danes: The Danish National Identity and Political Culture," *Comparative Studies in Society and History* 34 (1)(1992):13.

Chapter Six

1. This is a reference to Wendell Berry's famous treatise on American culture, *The Unsettling of America* (San Francisco: Sierra Club Books, 1977).

2. Lawrence Goodwyn, *Democratic Promise: The Populist Moment in America* (New York: Oxford University Press, 1976), 13–14. Goodwyn's account represents the most substantive work available on the Populist movement.

3. Ibid., 31–32.

4. Ibid., 96.

5. Ingolf Vogeler, *The Myth of the Family Farm: Agribusiness Dominance of U.S. Agriculture* (Boulder: Westview Press, 1981), 51.

6. Goodwyn, *Democratic Promise*, 360.

7. Paul Theobald, *Call School: Rural Education in the Midwest to 1918* (Carbondale: Southern Illinois University Press, 1995), 86.

8. Michael N. Johnson, "Nineteenth-Century Agrarian Populism and Twentieth-Century Communitarianism: Points of Contact and Contrast," *Peabody Journal of Education* 70 (summer 1995):86–104.

9. Ibid., 96–97.

10. Charles Eliot, "The Function of Education in a Democracy," in Jay Bennett et al., *Foundations of Educational Policy in the United States* (Needham Heights, Mass.: Ginn Press, 1989), 193.

11. Mabel Carney, *Country Schools and the Country Life Movement* (Chicago: Petersen and Co., 1912), 3.

12. *Report of the Commission on Country Life* (Chapel Hill: University of North Carolina Press, 1944), 30–31.

13. Wilbert L. Anderson, *The Country Town: A Study in Rural Evolution* (New York: Baker and Taylor, 1906), 6, 23; Liberty Hyde Bailey, *The Country Life Movement in the United States* (New York: Macmillan, 1911), 20.

14. Edward Allsworth Ross, *The Social Trend* (New York: Macmillan, 1922), 47.

15. Bailey, *The Country Life Movement*, 16.

16. A. E. Pickard, *Rural Education: A Complete Course of Study for Modern Rural Schools* (St. Paul: Webb Publishing, 1915), 209.

17. For examples, see William L. Bowers, *The Country Life Movement in America, 1900–1920* (Port Washington, N.Y.: Kennikat Press, 1974); David B. Danbom, *The Resisted Revolution: Urban America and the Industrialization of Agriculture, 1900–1930* (Ames: Iowa State University Press, 1979).

18. Mabel Carney, *Country Life and the Country School* (Chicago: Row, Peterson and Co., 1912), 177.

19. "What the President's Commission Is Doing," *American Farm Review* 1 (November 1908):4.

20. "Lo! The Poor Farmer," *Country Gentleman* 78 (September 1908):909–910.

21. These statistics and more are cited in Ronnie Dugger, "A Call to Citizens: Real Populists Please Stand Up," *Nation* 261 (August 14/21, 1995):159–164.

22. Wendell Berry, *What Are People For?* (San Francisco: North Point Press, 1990), 168.

23. Grant McConnell, *The Decline of Agrarian Democracy* (Berkeley: University of California Press, 1953), 36.

24. Ibid.

25. Ibid., 20. Clearly, corporate philanthropy was a key player in the development of agricultural extension, a process with obvious utility for growing agricultural support industries. The philanthropist Julius Rosenwald, for example, offered one thousand dollars to the first one hundred counties to employ a county agent.

26. Marty Strange, *Family Farming: A New Economic Vision* (Lincoln: University of Nebraska Press, 1988), 16.

27. Osha Gray Davidson, *Broken Heartland: The Rise of America's Rural Ghetto* (New York: Doubleday, 1990), 26.

28. Ibid., 29–30.

29. Seymour Martin Lipset, *Agrarian Socialism* (Berkeley: University of California Press, 1950), 111–112.

Chapter Seven

1. Joshua Meyrowitz, *No Sense of Place: The Impact of Electronic Media on Social Behavior* (New York: Oxford University Press, 1985).

2. I know of no more poignant description of this dynamic than Daniel Kemmis' chapter "Barn Raising" in *Community and the Politics of Place* (Norman: University of Oklahoma Press, 1990), 64–83.

3. Goodlad's address was reprinted in the *Journal of Moral Education* 21 (2)(1992):87–97.

4. Reinhold Niebuhr, *The Irony of American History* (New York: Charles Scribner's Sons, 1952), 63.

5. In the field of history, one can explore this supposition in Richard Hofstadter's famous work, *Anti-Intellectualism in American Life* (New York: Knopf, 1963). In the area of philosophy, one might look to our cultural slighting of epistemological issues in Cornel West's famous work *The American Evasion of Philosophy* (Madison: University of Wisconsin Press, 1989). In the field of education, Craig B. Howley, Aimee Howley, and Edwina D. Pendarvis' *Out of Our Minds: Anti-Intellectualism and Talent Development in American Schooling* (New York: Teachers College Press, 1995) represents the best, most systematic treatment of this theme.

6. Michael Fullan, *Change Forces: Probing the Depth of Educational Reform* (New York: Falmer Press, 1993), 24.

Chapter Eight

1. Until recent inroads were made by constructivists, even theories related to learning were unwittingly anchored in cultural assumptions about the primacy of the individual.

2. See, for example, Peter Drucker, *Managing the Future* (New York: Dutton, 1992), 108; and Peter Senge, *The Fifth Discipline* (New York: Doubleday, 1990), 139.

3. Michel de Montaigne, *Selected Essays*, trans. Donald Frame (New York: Walter J. Black, 1943), 48.

4. Alfie Kohn, *Punished by Rewards: The Trouble with Gold Stars, Incentive Plans, A's, Praise, and Other Bribes* (New York: Houghton Mifflin, 1993).

5. Forrest Gathercoal, *Judicious Discipline*, 3d ed. (San Francisco: Caddo Gap Press, 1994).

6. See, for instance, Arthur G. Powell, Eleanor Farrar, and David K. Cohen, *The Shopping Mall High School: Winners and Losers in the Educational Marketplace* (Boston: Houghton Mifflin, 1985).

7. Robert Shutes and Sandra Petersen, "Seven Reasons Why Textbooks Cannot Make a Curriculum," *NASSP Bulletin* 78 (November 1994):11–19.

8. Howard Gardner, *Frames of Mind: The Theory of Multiple Intelligences* (New York: Basic Books, 1983), and *The Unschooled Mind: How Children Think and How Schools Should Teach* (New York: Basic Books, 1991).

9. Paul A. Olson, *The Journey to Wisdom: Self-Education in Patristic and Medieval Literature* (University of Nebraska Press, 1995), 41–46.

Chapter Nine

1. The magnitude of farm tenancy rates suggests that this has been more a matter of necessity, and thus appearances, than a matter of fact.

2. See, for example, Lawrence C. Soley, *Leasing the Ivory Tower: The Corporate Takeover of Academia* (Boston: South End Press, 1995).

3. C. Wright Mills, *The Sociological Imagination* (New York: Grove Press, 1959), 226.

4. Howard Gardner, *Frames of Mind: The Theory of Multiple Intelligences* (New York: Basic Books, 1983).

About the Book and Author

Reaching all the way back to the classical and medieval past, *Teaching the Commons* chronicles ideas and resulting policies that have shaped contemporary rural life and living in much of the industrial West. The book examines philosophical assumptions and charts their evolution into conventional wisdom about how human beings should meet their needs, govern themselves, and educate their children. Further, this book examines how policies emanating from these assumptions have slowly eroded the vitality of rural communities, finding that if there is sufficient interest in saving what is left of rural America, an educational agenda at the local level needs to be embraced by America's rural schools.

Using concrete ideas generated in rural schools across the country, *Teaching the Commons* demonstrates that it is possible to simultaneously revitalize rural schools and communities. Through concerted curricular and pedagogical attention to place—the immediate locality—schools can contribute to rebuilding community in rural America on an educational foundation.

Arguing that vital, self-governing communities rather than self-interested individuals represent the greatest hope for American democracy, *Teaching the Commons* lays out an institutional foundation that would turn the cultivation of civic virtue into an educational goal every bit as important and attainable as education for success in the economic market.

Paul Theobald is associate dean of the College of Liberal Studies and director of the School of Education at the University of Wisconsin–La Crosse. He was formerly head of the Department of Teacher Education and coordinator of the Program for Rural School and Community Renewal at South Dakota State University in Brookings.

Index